One of the foremost dramatists of our time, Peter Shaffer was born in Liverpool and educated at St Paul's School and Trinity College, Cambridge. He had several varied jobs before earning fame as a playwright – working as a 'Bevin Boy' in the coal mines during the Second World War, in the acquisitions department of the New York Public Library and for the London music-publishing firm of Boosey & Hawkes.

His first big success came in 1958 with *Five Finger Exercise*. The play ran for nearly two years at the Comedy Theatre in London, won the *Evening Standard* Drama Award and was subsequently presented, with great acclaim, in New York City. Other Shaffer successes include *The Private Ear: The Public Eye* (which, like *Lettice and Lovage*, starred Maggie Smith and played at the Globe Theatre); *The Royal Hunt of the Sun*, an epic drama concerning the Spanish conquest of the Inca Empire; the hilarious farce, *Black Comedy*; *The Battle of Shrivings*; *Equus*, a sensational triumph in London and in New York where it received the 1975 Tony Award for Best Play of the Year; and *Amadeus*, which also won the same prize, as well as the 1979 *Evening Standard* Drama Award, the Plays and Players Award, and the London Theatre Critics' Award. Both these last mentioned plays boast the rare distinction of having run for over a thousand performances on Broadway and in 1984 the film of *Amadeus* won the Academy Award for both script and picture. His most recent plays are *Yonadab*, *Lettice and Lovage* which received the *Evening Standard* Drama Award for the best comedy of 1988, and *The Gift of the Gorgon*. Penguin publish a number of his plays. Peter Shaffer was awarded the CBE in the 1987 Birthday Honours List.

AMADEUS

A PLAY BY

PETER SHAFFER

PENGUIN BOOKS

For Robert with Love

PENGUIN BOOKS

Published by the Penguin Group
Penguin Books Ltd, 27 Wrights Lane, London W8 5TZ, England
Penguin Books USA Inc., 375 Hudson Street, New York, New York 10014, USA
Penguin Books Australia Ltd, Ringwood, Victoria, Australia
Penguin Books Canada Ltd, 10 Alcorn Avenue, Toronto, Ontario, Canada M4V 3B2
Penguin Books (NZ) Ltd, 182–190 Wairau Road, Auckland 10, New Zealand

Penguin Books Ltd, Registered Offices: Harmondsworth, Middlesex, England

First published in Great Britain by André Deutsch 1980
Revised edition published in Penguin Books 1981
Reprinted with minor revisions and a postscript 1993
1 3 5 7 9 10 8 6 4 2

Printed in England by Clays Ltd, St Ives plc
Filmset in Monophoto Bembo

AUTHOR'S NOTES

THE SET

Amadeus can and should be played in a variety of settings. What is described in this text is to a large extent based on the exquisite formulation found for the play by the designer John Bury, conjured into being by the director, Peter Hall. I was of course in enthusiastic agreement with his formulation, and set it down here with their permission as a tribute to their exquisite work.

The set consisted basically of a handsome rectangle of patterned wood, its longest sides leading away from the viewer, set into a stage of ice-blue plastic. This surface shifted beguilingly under various lights played upon it, to show gunmetal grey, or azure, or emerald green, and reflected the actors standing upon it. The entire design was undeniably modern, yet it suggested without self-consciousness the age of the Rococo. Costumes and objects were sumptuously of the period, and should always be so wherever the play is produced.

The rectangle largely represented interiors: especially those of Salieri's salon; Mozart's last apartment; assorted reception rooms, and opera houses. At the back stood a grand proscenium sporting gilded cherubs blowing huge trumpets, and supporting grand curtains of sky blue, which could rise and part to reveal an enclosed space almost the width of the area downstage. Into this space superb backdrops were flown, and superb projections thrown, to show the scarlet boxes of theatres, the black shape of the guillotine, or a charming white Masonic Lodge copied from a china plate. In it the audience could see an eighteenth-century street at night (cunningly enlarged from the lid of Mozart's own curious snuff-box) or a vast wall of gold

5

mirrors with an immense golden fireplace, representing the encrusted Palace of Schönbrunn. In it also appeared silhouettes of scandal-mongering citizens of Vienna, or the formal figures of the Emperor Joseph II of Austria and his brocaded courtiers. This wonderful up-stage space, which was in effect an immense Rococo peepshow, will be referred to throughout this text as the Light Box.

On stage, before the lights are lowered in the theatre, four objects are to be seen by the audience. To the left, on the wooden rectangle, stands a small table, bearing an empty cake-stand and a small handbell. In the centre, further upstage and also on the wood, stands an empty wheelchair of the eighteenth century, with its back to us. To the right, on the reflecting plastic, stands a beautiful fortepiano in a marquetry case. Above the stage is suspended a large chandelier showing many globes of opaque glass.

All directions will be given from the viewpoint of the audience.

Changes of time and place are indicated throughout by changes of light.

In reading the text it must be remembered that the action is wholly continuous. Its fluidity is ensured by the use of servants played by actors in eighteenth-century livery, whose role it is to move the furniture and carry on props with ease and correctness, while the action proceeds around them. Through a pleasant paradox of theatre their constant coming and going, bearing tables, chairs or cloaks, should render them virtually invisible, and certainly unremarkable. This will aid the play to be acted throughout in its proper manner: with the sprung line, gracefulness and energy for which Mozart is so especially celebrated.

The asterisks which now and then divide the page indicate changes of scene: but there is to be no interruption. The scenes must flow into one another without pause from the beginning to the end of the play.

P.S.

6

Amadeus was first presented by the National Theatre in London on 2 November 1979 with the following cast:

THE 'VENTICELLI'	Dermot Crowley
	Donald Gee
VALET TO SALIERI	Philip Locke
ANTONIO SALIERI	Paul Scofield
JOHANN KILIAN VON STRACK	Basil Henson
COUNT ORSINI-ROSENBERG	Andrew Cruickshank
BARON VAN SWIETEN	Nicholas Selby
CONSTANZE WEBER	Felicity Kendal
WOLFGANG AMADEUS MOZART	Simon Callow
MAJOR-DOMO	William Sleigh
JOSEPH II, EMPEROR OF AUSTRIA	John Normington
SERVANTS	Nik Forster, David Morris, Louis Selwyn, Steven Slater
CITIZENS OF VIENNA	Glyn Baker, Nigel Bellairs, Leo Dove, Jane Evers, Susan Gilmore, Robin McDonald, Peggy Marshall, Robin Meredith, Ann Sedgwick, Glenn Williams

Director: Peter Hall
Design and Lighting: John Bury
Assistant Designer: Sue Jenkinson
Music by Mozart and Salieri
Music Direction: Harrison Birtwistle
Fortepiano played by Christopher Kite

This is a revised version of *Amadeus* first produced at the Broadhurst Theater, New York City, on 17 December 1980. It starred Ian McKellen as Salieri, Tim Curry as Mozart, and Jane Seymour as Constanze. The Director was Peter Hall.

CHARACTERS

ANTONIO SALIERI	
WOLFGANG AMADEUS MOZART	
CONSTANZE WEBER	Wife to Mozart
JOSEPH II	Emperor of Austria
COUNT JOHANN KILIAN VON STRACK	Groom of the Imperial Chamber
COUNT FRANZ ORSINI-ROSENBERG	Director of the Imperial Opera
BARON GOTTFRIED VAN SWIETEN	Prefect of the Imperial Library
TWO 'VENTICELLI'	'Little Winds': purveyors of information, gossip and rumour
MAJOR-DOMO	
SALIERI'S VALET	(Silent part)
SALIERI'S COOK	(Silent part)
TERESA SALIERI	Wife of Salieri (silent part)
KATHERINA CAVALIERI	Salieri's pupil (silent part)
KAPELLMEISTER BONNO	(Silent part)
CITIZENS OF VIENNA	

The CITIZENS OF VIENNA also play the SERVANTS who move furniture and bring on props as required, and TERESA SALIERI and KATHERINA CAVALIERI, neither of whom have any lines to speak.

The action of the play takes place in Vienna in November 1823, and, in recall, the decade 1781–1791.

8

ACT I

Darkness.
Savage whispers fill the theatre. We can distinguish nothing at first from this snake-like hissing save the word Salieri! *repeated here, there and everywhere around the theatre.*
Also, the barely distinguishable word Assassin!
The whispers overlap and increase in volume, slashing the air with wicked intensity. Then the light grows upstage to reveal the silhouettes of men and women dressed in the top hats and skirts of the early nineteenth century — CITIZENS OF VIENNA, *all crowded together in the Light Box, and uttering their scandal.*

WHISPERERS: *Salieri!* ... *Salieri!* ... *Salieri!*
   [*Downstage in the wheelchair, with his back to us, sits an old man. We can just see, as the light grows a little brighter, the top of his head encased in an old cap, and perhaps the shawl wrapped around his shoulders.*]
Salieri! ... *Salieri!* ... *Salieri!*
   [*Two middle-aged gentlemen hurry in from either side, also wearing the long cloaks and tall hats of the period. These are the* TWO VENTICELLI: *purveyors of fact, rumour and gossip throughout the play. They speak rapidly — in this first appearance extremely rapidly — so that the scene has the air of a fast and dreadful Overture. Sometimes they speak to each other; sometimes to us — but always with the urgency of men who have ever been first with the news.*]

9

VENTICELLO 1: I don't believe it.
VENTICELLO 2: I don't believe it.
VENTICELLO 1: I don't believe it.
VENTICELLO 2: I don't believe it.
WHISPERERS: *Salieri!*

VENTICELLO 1: They say.
VENTICELLO 2: I hear.
VENTICELLO 1: I hear.
VENTICELLO 2: They say.
VENTICELLO 1 and VENTICELLO 2: *I don't believe it!*
WHISPERERS: *Salieri!*

VENTICELLO 1: The whole city is talking.
VENTICELLO 2: You hear it all over.
VENTICELLO 1: The cafés.
VENTICELLO 2: The Opera.
VENTICELLO 1: The Prater.
VENTICELLO 2: The gutter.
VENTICELLO 1: They say even Metternich repeats it.
VENTICELLO 2: They say even Beethoven, his old pupil.
VENTICELLO 1: But why now?
VENTICELLO 2: After so long?
VENTICELLO 1: Thirty-two years!
VENTICELLO 1 and VENTICELLO 2: *I don't believe it!*
WHISPERERS: SALIERI!

VENTICELLO 1: They say he shouts it out all day!
VENTICELLO 2: I hear he cries it out all night!
VENTICELLO 1: Stays in his apartments.
VENTICELLO 2: Never goes out.
VENTICELLO 1: Not for a year now.
VENTICELLO 2: Longer. Longer.
VENTICELLO 1: Must be seventy.
VENTICELLO 2: Older. Older.
VENTICELLO 1: Antonio Salieri –
VENTICELLO 2: The famous musician –

VENTICELLO 1: Shouting it aloud!

VENTICELLO 2: Crying it aloud!

VENTICELLO 1: Impossible.

VENTICELLO 2: Incredible.

VENTICELLO 1: I don't believe it!

VENTICELLO 2: I don't believe it!

WHISPERERS: SALIERI!

VENTICELLO 1: I know who *started* the tale!

VENTICELLO 2: *I* know who started the tale!

[*Two old men – one thin and dry, one very fat – detach themselves from the crowd at the back, and walk downstage, on either side: Salieri's* VALET *and* PASTRY COOK.]

VENTICELLO 1 [*indicating him*]: The old man's valet!

VENTICELLO 2 [*indicating him*]: The old man's cook!

VENTICELLO 1: The valet hears him shouting!

VENTICELLO 2: The cook hears him crying!

VENTICELLO 1: What a story!

VENTICELLO 2: What a scandal!

[*The* VENTICELLI *move quickly upstage, one on either side, and each collects a silent informant.* VENTICELLO 1 *walks down eagerly with the* VALET; VENTICELLO 2 *walks down eagerly with the* COOK.]

VENTICELLO 1 [*to* VALET]: What does he say, your master?

VENTICELLO 2 [*to* COOK]: What *exactly* does he cry, the Kapellmeister?

VENTICELLO 1: Alone in his house –

VENTICELLO 2: All day and all night –

VENTICELLO 1: What sins does he shout?

VENTICELLO 2: The old fellow –

VENTICELLO 1: The recluse –

VENTICELLO 2: What horrors have you heard?

VENTICELLO 1 and VENTICELLO 2: Tell us! Tell us! Tell us at once! What does he cry? What does he cry? *What does he cry?*

[VALET *and* COOK *gesture towards* SALIERI.]

SALIERI [*in a great cry*]: MOZART!!!

[*Silence.*]

VENTICELLO 1 [*whispering*]: Mozart!
VENTICELLO 2 [*whispering*]: Mozart!
SALIERI: *Perdonami, Mozart! Il tuo assassino ti chiede perdono!*
VENTICELLO 1 [*in disbelief*]: Pardon, Mozart!
VENTICELLO 2 [*in disbelief*]: Pardon your assassin!
VENTICELLO 1 and VENTICELLO 2: *God preserve us!*

SALIERI: *Pietà, Mozart. Mozart, pietà!*
VENTICELLO 1: Mercy, Mozart!
VENTICELLO 2: Mozart, have mercy!
VENTICELLO 1: He speaks in Italian when excited!
VENTICELLO 2: German when not!
VENTICELLO 1: *Perdonami, Mozart!*
VENTICELLO 2: Pardon your assassin!
> [*The* VALET *and the* COOK *walk to either side of the stage, and stand still. Pause. The* VENTICELLI *cross themselves, deeply shocked.*]
VENTICELLO 1: There was talk once before, you know.
VENTICELLO 2: Thirty-two years ago.
VENTICELLO 1: When Mozart was dying.
VENTICELLO 2: He claimed he'd been poisoned.
VENTICELLO 1: Some said he accused a man.
VENTICELLO 2: Some said that man was Salieri.
VENTICELLO 1: But no one believed it.
VENTICELLO 2: They *knew* what he died of!
VENTICELLO 1: Syphilis, surely.
VENTICELLO 2: Like everybody else.
> [*Pause.*]
VENTICELLO 1 [*slyly*]: But what if Mozart was right?
VENTICELLO 2: If he really *was* murdered?
VENTICELLO 1: And by him. Our First Kapellmeister!
VENTICELLO 2: Antonio Salieri!
VENTICELLO 1: It can't possibly be true.
VENTICELLO 2: It's not actually credible.
VENTICELLO 1: Because *why*?
VENTICELLO 2: Because why?

VENTICELLO I and VENTICELLO 2: *Why on earth would he do it?*
VENTICELLO I: Our First Royal Kapellmeister —
VENTICELLO 2: Murder his inferior?
VENTICELLO I: And why confess *now*?
VENTICELLO 2: After thirty-two years!
WHISPERERS: SALIERI!

SALIERI: *Mozart! Mozart! Perdonami!* ... *Il tuo assassino ti chiede perdono!*
  [*Pause. They look at him — then at each other.*]
VENTICELLO I: What do you think?
VENTICELLO 2: What do you think?
VENTICELLO I: I don't believe it!
VENTICELLO 2: *I* don't believe it!
VENTICELLO I: All the same ...
VENTICELLO 2: Is it just possible?
VENTICELLO I and VENTICELLO 2 [*whispering*]: *Did he do it after all?!*
WHISPERERS: SALIERI!

  [*The* VENTICELLI *go off. The* VALET *and the* COOK *remain, on either side of the stage.* SALIERI *swivels his wheelchair around and stares at us. We see a man of seventy in an old stained dressing-robe, shawled. He rises and squints at the audience as if trying to see it.*]

*   *   *

SALIERI'S APARTMENTS
NOVEMBER 1823. THE SMALL HOURS

SALIERI [*calling to audience*]: *Vi Saluto! Ombri del Futuro! Antonio Salieri — a vostro servizio!*

  [*A clock outside in the street strikes three.*]

I can almost see you in your ranks — waiting for your turn to live. Ghosts of the Future! Be visible. I beg you. Be visible. Come to this dusty old room – this time, the smallest hours of dark November, eighteen hundred and twenty-three – and be my Confessors! Will you not enter this place and stay with me till dawn? Just till dawn – till six o'clock!

WHISPERERS: *Salieri!* ... *Salieri!* ...

[*The curtains slowly descend on the* CITIZENS OF VIENNA. *Faint images of long windows are projected on the silk.*]

SALIERI: Can you hear them? Vienna is a City of Slander. Everyone tells tales here: even my servants. I keep only two now – [*He indicates them*] – they've been with me ever since I came here, fifty years ago. The Keeper of the Razor: the Maker of the Cakes. One keeps me tidy, the other keeps me full. Tonight, I gave them instructions they never heard before. [*To them*] 'Leave me, both of you! Tonight I do not go to bed at all!'

[*They react in surprise.*]

'Return here tomorrow morning at six precisely – to shave, to feed your capricious master!' [*He smiles at them both and claps his hands in gentle dismissal.*] Via. Via, via, via! Grazie!

[*They bow, bewildered, and leave the stage.*]

How surprised they were! ... They'll be even more surprised tomorrow: indeed they will! [*He peers hard at the audience, trying to see it.*] Oh, won't you appear? I need you – desperately! This is now the last hour of my life. Those about to die implore you! What must I do to make you visible? Raise you up in the flesh to be my last, last audience? ... Does it take an Invocation? That's how it's always done in opera! Ah yes, of course: that's it. An *Invocation!* The only way [*He rises.*] Let me try to conjure you *now* – Ghosts of the distant Future – so that I can see you.

[*He gets out of the wheelchair and huddles over to the fortepiano. He stands at the instrument and begins to sing in a high cracked voice, interrupting himself at the end of each sentence with figurations on the keyboard in the manner of a* recitativo secco. *During this the house lights slowly come up to illuminate the audience.*]

[*Singing*]

Ghosts of the Future!

Shades of Time to come!
So much more unavoidable than those of Time gone by!
Appear with what sympathy Incarnation may endow you!
Appear You –
The yet-to-be-born!
The yet-to-hate!
The yet-to-*kill*!
Appear – Posterity!

[*The light on the audience reaches its maximum. It stays like this during all of the following.*]

[*Speaking again*] There. It worked. I can see you! That is the result of proper training. I was taught invocation by Chevalier Gluck, who was a true master at it. He had to be. In his day that is what people went to the opera for: the raising of Gods, and Ghosts ... Nowadays, since Rossini became the rage, they prefer to watch the escapades of hairdressers.

[*Pause.*]

Scusate. Invocation is an exhausting business! I need refreshment. [*He goes to the cake-stand.*] It's a little repellent, I admit – but actually the first sin I have to confess to you is Gluttony. Sticky gluttony at that. Infantine – Italian gluttony! The truth is that all my life I have never been able to conquer a lust for the sweetmeats of northern Italy where I was born. From the ages of three to seventy-three my entire career has been conducted to the taste of almonds sprinkled with sifted sugar. [*Lustfully*] Veronese biscuits! Milanese macaroons! Snow dumplings with pistachio sauce! [*Pause*] Do not judge me too harshly for this. All men harbour patriotic feelings of some kind ... Of course I was born in 1750, when no man of sophistication would have dreamed of talking about Love of Country, or Native Earth. We were men of Europe, and that was enough. My parents were provincial subjects of the Austrian Empire, and perfectly happy to be so. A Lombardy merchant and his Lombardy wife. Their notion of Place was the tiny town of Legnago – which I could not wait to leave. Their notion of God was a superior Hapsburg emperor inhabiting a heaven only slightly further off than Vienna. All they required of Him was to protect commerce and keep them forever unnoticed – preserved in mediocrity. My own requirements were very different.

[*Pause.*]

I wanted Fame. Not to deceive you. I wanted to *blaze*, like a comet, across the firmament of Europe. Yet only in one especial way. Music. Absolute music! A note of music is either right or wrong – *absolutely*! Not even Time can alter that: music is God's art. [*Excited by the recollection*] Already when I was ten a spray of sounded notes would make me dizzy almost to falling! By twelve I was humming my arias and anthems to the Lord. My one desire was to join all the composers who had celebrated His glory through the long Italian past! . . . Every Sunday I saw Him in church, painted on the flaking wall. I don't mean Christ. The Christs of Lombardy are simpering sillies with lambkins on their sleeves. No: I mean an old candle-smoked God in a mulberry robe, staring at the world with dealer's eyes. Tradesmen had put him up there. Those eyes made bargains, real and irreversible. 'You give me so – I'll give you so! No more. No less!' [*He eats a sweet biscuit in his excitement.*] The night before I left Legnago for ever I went to see Him and made a bargain with Him myself! I was a sober sixteen, filled with a desperate sense of right. I knelt before the God of Bargains, and I prayed through the mouldering plaster with all my soul.

[*He kneels. The house lights go down.*]

'Signore, let me be a composer! Grant me sufficient fame to enjoy it. In return I will live with virtue. I will strive to better the lot of my fellows. And I will honour You with much music all the days of my life!' As I said Amen, I saw his eyes flare. [*As 'God'*] '*Bene*. Go forth Antonio. Serve Me and Mankind – and you will be blessed!' . . . '*Grazie!*' I called back. 'I am Your servant for life!'

[*He gets to his feet again.*]

The very next day, a family friend suddenly appeared – out of the blue – took me off to Vienna, and paid for me to study music!

[*Pause.*]

Shortly afterwards I met the Emperor, who favoured me – and was to advance my career beyond all expectations! *Clearly my bargain had been accepted!*

[*Pause.*]

The same year I left Italy, a young prodigy was touring Europe. A miraculous virtuoso aged ten years. Wolfgang Amadeus Mozart.

[*Pause. He smiles at the audience.*

Pause.]

And now – Gracious Ladies! Obliging Gentlemen! I present to you – for one performance only – my last composition, entitled *The Death of Mozart*, or *Did I Do It?* ... dedicated to Posterity on this – the last night of my life!

[*He bows deeply, undoing as he does so the buttons of his old dressing-robe. When he straightens himself – divesting himself of this drab outer garment and his cap – he is a young man in the prime of life, wearing a sky-blue coat and the elegant decent clothes of a successful composer of the seventeen-eighties.*]

*   *   *

TRANSFORMATION TO THE EIGHTEENTH CENTURY

[*Music sounds softly in the background: a serene piece for strings by Salieri.* SERVANTS *enter. One takes away the dressing-robe and shawl; another places on the table a wig-stand bearing a powdered wig; a third brings on a chair and places it at the left, upstage.*

At the back the blue curtains rise and part to show the EMPEROR JOSEPH II *and his Court bathed in golden light, against a golden background of mirrors and an immense golden fireplace. His Majesty is seated, holding a rolled paper, listening to the music. Also listening are* COUNT VON STRACK; COUNT ORSINI-ROSENBERG; BARON VAN SWIETEN; *and an anonymous* PRIEST *dressed in a soutane. An old wigged courtier enters and takes his place at the keyboard:* KAPELLMEISTER BONNO. SALIERI *takes his wig from the stand.*]

SALIERI [*in a young man's voice: vigorous and confident*]: The place throughout is Vienna. The year — to begin with — seventeen eighty-one. The age still that of the Enlightenment: that clear time before the guillotine fell in France and cut all our lives in half. I am thirty-one. Already a prolific composer to the Hapsburg Court. I own a respectable house and a respectable wife — Teresa.

[*Enter* TERESA: *a padded placid lady who seats herself uprightly in the chair upstage.*]

I do not mock her, I assure you. I required only one quality in a domestic companion — lack of fire. And in that omission Teresa was conspicuous. [*Ceremoniously he puts on his powdered wig.*] I also had a prize pupil: Katherina Cavalieri.

[KATHERINA *swirls on from the opposite side: a beautiful girl of twenty. The music becomes vocal: faintly, we hear a soprano singing a concert aria. Like* TERESA's, KATHERINA's *part is mute — but as she enters she stands by the fortepiano, and energetically mimes her rapturous singing. At the keyboard old* BONNO *accompanies her appreciatively.*]

SALIERI: She was later to become the best singer of her Age. But at that time she was mainly a bubbling student with merry eyes and a sweet, eatable mouth. I was very much in love with Katherina — or at least in lust. But because of my vow to God, I was entirely faithful to my wife. I had never laid a finger upon the girl — except occasionally to depress her diaphragm in the way of teaching her to sing. My ambition burned with an unquenchable flame. Its chief goal was the post of First Royal Kapellmeister, then held by Giuseppe Bonno — [*indicating him*] — seventy years old, and apparently immortal.

[*All on stage, save* SALIERI, *suddenly freeze. He speaks very directly to the audience.*]

You, when you come, will be told that we musicians of the eighteenth century were no better than servants: the willing slaves of the well-to-do. This is quite true. It is also quite false. Yes, we were servants. But we were learned servants! And we used our learning to celebrate men's average lives!

[*A grander music sounds. The* EMPEROR *remains seated, but the other four men in the Light Box —* VON STRACK, ORSINI-ROSENBERG, VAN SWIETEN *and the* PRIEST *— come slowly out on to the main stage and process imposingly down it, and around it, and up it again to return to their places. Only the* PRIEST *goes off, as do* TERESA *on her side, and* KATHERINA *on hers.*]

[*Over this*] We took unremarkable men: usual bankers, run-of-the-mill priests, ordinary soldiers and statesmen and wives — and sacramentalized their mediocrity. We smoothed their noons with strings *divisi*! We pierced their nights with *chittarini*! We gave them processions for their strutting — serenades for their rutting — high horns for their hunting, and drums for their wars! Trumpets sounded when they entered the world, and trombones groaned when they left it! The savour of their days remains behind because of *us*, our music still remembered while their politics are long forgotten.

[*The* EMPEROR *hands his rolled paper to* VON STRACK *and goes off. In the Light Box are left standing, like three icons,* ORSINI-ROSENBERG, *plump and supercilious, aged sixty;* VON STRACK, *stiff and proper, aged fifty-five;* VAN SWIETEN, *cultivated and serious, aged fifty. The lights go down on them a little.*]

Tell me, before you call us servants, who served whom? And who I wonder, in your generations, will immortalize *you*?

[*The* TWO VENTICELLI *come on quickly downstage, from either side. They are now bewigged also, and are dressed well, in the style of the late eighteenth century. Their manner is more confidential than before.*]

VENTICELLO I [*to* SALIERI]: Sir!
VENTICELLO 2 [*to* SALIERI]: Sir!
VENTICELLO I: Sir. Sir.
VENTICELLO 2: Sir. Sir. Sir!

[SALIERI *bids them wait for a second.*]

SALIERI: I was the most successful young musician in the city of musicians. And now suddenly, without warning —

[*They approach him eagerly, from either side.*]

VENTICELLO 1: Mozart!

VENTICELLO 2: Mozart!

VENTICELLO 1 and VENTICELLO 2: *Mozart has come!*

SALIERI: These are my *Venticelli*. My 'Little Winds', as I call them. [*He gives each a coin from his pocket.*] The secret of successful living in a large city is always to know to the minute what is being done behind your back.

VENTICELLO 1: He's left Salzburg.

VENTICELLO 2: Means to give concerts.

VENTICELLO 1: Asking for subscribers.

SALIERI: I'd known of him for years, of course. Tales of his prowess were told all over Europe.

VENTICELLO 1: They say he wrote his first symphony at five.

VENTICELLO 2: I hear his first concerto at four

VENTICELLO 1: A full opera at fourteen.

SALIERI [*to them*]: How old is he now?

VENTICELLO 2: Twenty-five.

SALIERI [*carefully*]: And how long is he remaining?

VENTICELLO 1: He's not departing.

VENTICELLO 2: He's here to stay.

[*The* VENTICELLI *glide off.*]

★   ★   ★

THE PALACE OF SCHÖNBRUNN

[*Lights come up on the three stiff figures of* ORSINI-ROSENBERG, VON STRACK *and* VAN SWIETEN, *standing upstage in the Light Box. The* CHAMBERLAIN *hands the paper he has received from the Emperor to the* DIRECTOR OF THE OPERA. SALIERI *remains downstage.*]

VON STRACK [*to* ORSINI-ROSENBERG]: You are required to commission a comic opera in German from Herr Mozart.

SALIERI [*to audience*]: Johann von Strack. Royal Chamberlain. A Court official to his collar bone.

ROSENBERG [*loftily*]: Why in German? Italian is the only possible language for opera!

SALIERI: Count Orsini-Rosenberg. Director of the Opera. Benevolent to all things Italian – especially myself.

VON STRACK [*stiffly*]: The idea of a National Opera is dear to His Majesty's heart. He desires to hear pieces in good plain German.

VAN SWIETEN: Yes, but why comic? It is not the function of music to be funny.

SALIERI: Baron van Swieten. Prefect of the Imperial Library. Ardent Freemason. Yet to find anything funny. Known for his enthusiasm for old-fashioned music as 'Lord Fugue'.

VAN SWIETEN: I heard last week a remarkable *serious* opera from Mozart: *Idomeneo, King of Crete*.

ROSENBERG: I heard that too. A young fellow trying to impress beyond his abilities. Too much spice. Too many notes.

VONSTRACK [*firmly, to* ORSINI-ROSENBERG]: Nevertheless, kindly convey the commission to him today.

ROSENBERG [*taking the paper reluctantly*]: I believe we are going to have trouble with this young man.

[ORSINI-ROSENBERG *leaves the Light Box and strolls down the stage to* SALIERI.]

ROSENBERG: He was a child prodigy. That always spells trouble. His father is Leopold Mozart, a bad-tempered Salzburg musician who dragged the boy endlessly round Europe making him play the keyboard blindfold, with one finger, and that sort of thing. [*To* SALIERI] All prodigies are hateful – *non è vero, Compositore?*

SALIERI: *Divengono sempre sterili con gli anni.*

ROSENBERG: *Precisamente. Precisamente.*

VON STRACK [*calling suspiciously*]: What are you saying?

ROSENBERG [*airily*]: Nothing, Herr Chamberlain! ... *Niente*, Signor Pomposo! ... [*He strolls on out.*]

[VON STRACK *strides off irritated.* VAN SWIETEN *now comes downstage.*]

VAN SWIETEN: We meet tomorrow, I believe, on your committee to devise pensions for old musicians.

SALIERI [*deferentially*]: It's most gracious of you to attend, Baron.

VAN SWIETEN: You're a worthy man, Salieri. You should join our Brotherhood of Masons. We would welcome you warmly.

SALIERI: I would be honoured, Baron!

VAN SWIETEN: If you wished I could arrange initiation into my Lodge.

SALIERI: That would be more than my due.

VAN SWIETEN: Nonsense. We embrace men of talent of all conditions. I may invite young Mozart also: dependent on the impression he makes.

SALIERI [*bowing*]: Of course, Baron.

[VAN SWIETEN *goes out.*]

[*To audience*] Honour indeed. In those days almost every man of influence in Vienna was a Mason — and the Baron's Lodge by far the most fashionable. As for young Mozart, I confess I was alarmed by his coming. Not by the commission of a comic opera, even though I myself was then attempting one called *The Chimney Sweep*. No, what worried me were reports about the man himself. He was praised altogether too much.

[*The* VENTICELLI *hurry in from either side.*]

VENTICELLO 1: Such gaiety of spirit!

VENTICELLO 2: Such ease of manner!

VENTICELLO 1: Such natural charm!

SALIERI [*to the* VENTICELLI]: Really? Where does he live?

VENTICELLO 1: Peter Platz.

VENTICELLO 2: Number eleven.

VENTICELLO 1: The landlady is Madame Weber.

VENTICELLO 2: A real bitch.

VENTICELLO 1: Takes in male lodgers, and has a tribe of daughters.

VENTICELLO 2: Mozart is after one of them.

VENTICELLO 1: Constanze.

VENTICELLO 2: Flighty little piece!

VENTICELLO 1: Her mother's pushing marriage.

VENTICELLO 2: His *father* isn't!

VENTICELLO 1: Daddy is worried sick!

VENTICELLO 2: Writes him every day from Salzburg!

SALIERI [*to them*]: I want to meet him. What houses does he visit?

VENTICELLO 1: He'll be at the Baroness Waldstädten's tomorrow night.

SALIERI: *Grazie.*

VENTICELLO 2: Some of his music is to be played.

SALIERI [*to both*]: *Restiamo in contatto.*

VENTICELLO 1 and VENTICELLO 2: *Certamente, Signore!*
    [*They go off.*]

SALIERI [*to audience*]: So to the Baroness Waldstädten's I went. That night changed my life.

*   *   *

THE LIBRARY OF THE BARONESS WALDSTÄDTEN

[*In the Light Box, two elegantly curtained windows surrounded by handsome subdued wallpaper.*
Two SERVANTS *bring on a large table loaded with cakes and desserts. Two more carry on a grand high-backed wing-chair, which they place ceremoniously downstage at the left.*]

SALIERI [*to audience*]: I entered the library to take first a little refreshment. My generous hostess always put out the most delicious confections in that room whenever she knew I was coming. *Sorbetti* – *caramelli* – and most especially a miraculous *crema al mascarpone* – which is simply cream cheese mixed with granulated sugar and suffused with rum – which was totally irresistible!
    [*He takes a little bowl of it from the cake-stand and sits in the wing-chair, facing out front. Thus seated, he is invisible to anyone entering from upstage.*]
I had just sat down in a high-backed chair to consume this paradisal

dish — unobservable as it happened to anyone who might come in.

[*Offstage, noises are heard.*]

CONSTANZE [*off*]: Squeak! Squeak! Squeak!

[CONSTANZE *runs on from upstage: a pretty girl in her early twenties, full of high spirits. At this second she is pretending to be a mouse. She runs across the stage in her gay party dress, and hides under the fortepiano.*

Suddenly a small, pallid, large-eyed man in a showy wig and a showy set of clothes runs in after her and freezes — centre — as a cat would freeze, hunting a mouse. This is WOLFGANG AMADEUS MOZART. *As we get to know him through his next scenes, we discover several things about him: he is an extremely restless man, his hands and feet in almost continuous motion; his voice is light and high; and he is possessed of an unforgettable giggle — piercing and infantile.*]

MOZART: Miaouw!

CONSTANZE [*betraying where she is*]: Squeak!

MOZART: Miaouw! Miaouw! Miaouw!

[*The composer drops on all fours and, wrinkling his face, begins spitting and stalking his prey. The mouse — giggling with excitement — breaks her cover and dashes across the floor. The cat pursues. Almost at the chair where* SALIERI *sits concealed, the mouse turns at bay. The cat stalks her — nearer and nearer — in its knee-breeches and elaborate coat.*]

I'm going to pounce-bounce! I'm going to scrunch-munch! I'm going to chew-poo my little mouse-wouse! I'm going to tear her to bits with my paws–claws!

CONSTANZE: No!

MOZART: Paws–claws! Paws–claws! ... OHH!

[*He falls on her. She screams.*]

SALIERI [*to audience*]: Before I could rise, it had become difficult to do so.

MOZART: I'm going to bite you in half with my fangs-wangs! My little Stanzerl-wanzerl-banzerl!

[*She giggles delightedly, lying prone beneath him.*]

You're trembling! ... I think you're frightened of puss-wuss! ...

I think you're scared to death! [*Intimately*] I think you're going to shit yourself!

[*She squeals, but is not really shocked.*]

MOZART: In a moment it's going to be on the floor!

CONSTANZE: Ssh! Someone'll hear you!

[*He imitates the noise of a fart.*]

Stop it, Wolferl! Ssh!

MOZART: Here it comes now! I can hear it *coming*! ... Oh what a melancholy note! Something's dropping from your boat!

[*Another fart noise, slower.* CONSTANZE *shrieks with amusement.*]

CONSTANZE: Stop it now! It's stupid! Really *stupid*!

[SALIERI *sits appalled.*]

MOZART: Hey — Hey — what's Trazom!

CONSTANZE: What?

MOZART: T-R-A-Z-O-M. What's that mean?

CONSTANZE: How should *I* know?

MOZART: It's Mozart spelt backwards — shit-wit! If you ever married me, you'd be Constanze Trazom.

CONSTANZE: No, I wouldn't.

MOZART: Yes, you would. Because I'd want everything backwards once I was married. I'd want to lick my wife's arse instead of her face.

CONSTANZE: You're not going to lick anything at this rate. Your father's never going to give his consent to us.

[*The sense of fun deserts him instantly.*]

MOZART: And who cares about his consent?

CONSTANZE: *You* do. You care very much. You wouldn't do it without it.

MOZART: Wouldn't I?

CONSTANZE: No, you wouldn't. Because you're too scared of him. I know what he says about me. [*Solemn voice*] 'If you marry that dreadful girl, you'll end up lying on straw with beggars for children.'

MOZART [*impulsively*]: Marry me!

CONSTANZE: Don't be silly.

MOZART: Marry me!

CONSTANZE: Are you serious?

MOZART [*defiantly*]: Yes! ... Answer me this minute: yes or no! Say yes, then I can go home, climb into bed – shit over the mattress and shout 'I *did* it!'

[*He rolls on top of her delightedly, uttering his high whinnying giggle. The* MAJOR-DOMO *of the house stalks in, upstage.*]

MAJOR-DOMO [*imperviously*]: Her Ladyship is ready to commence.

MOZART: Ah! ... Yes! ... Good! [*He picks himself up, embarrassed, and helps* CONSTANZE *to rise. With an attempt at dignity*] Come, my dear. The music waits!

CONSTANZE [*suppressing giggles*]: Oh, by all means – Herr Trazom! [*He takes her arm. They prance off together, followed by the disapproving* MAJOR-DOMO.]

SALIERI [*shaken: to audience*]: And then, right away, the concert began. I heard it through the door – some Serenade: at first only vaguely – too horrified to attend. But presently the sound insisted – a solemn Adagio in E flat.

[*The Adagio from the Serenade for Thirteen Wind Instruments (K.361) begins to sound. Quietly and quite slowly, seated in the wing-chair,* SALIERI *speaks over the music.*]

It started simply enough: just a pulse in the lowest registers – bassoons and basset horns – like a rusty squeezebox. It would have been comic except for the slowness, which gave it instead a sort of serenity. And then suddenly, high above it, sounded a single note on the oboe.

[*We hear it.*]

It hung there unwavering – piercing me through – till breath could hold it no longer, and a clarinet withdrew it out of me, and sweetened it into a phrase of such delight it had me trembling. The light flickered in the room. My eyes clouded! [*With ever-increasing emotion and vigour*] The squeezebox groaned louder, and over it the higher instruments wailed and warbled, throwing lines of sound around me – long lines of pain around and through me – Ah, the pain! Pain as I had never known it. I called up to my sharp old God '*What is this? ... What?!*' But the squeezebox went on and on, and the pain cut deeper into my shaking head until suddenly I was running –

[*He bolts out of the chair and runs across the stage in a fever, to a corner, down right. Behind him in the Light Box the Library fades into a street scene at night: small houses under a rent sky. The music continues, fainter, underneath.*]

– dashing through the side-door, stumbling downstairs into the street, into the cold night, gasping for life. [*Calling up in agony*] '*What?! What is this? Tell me, Signore!* What is this *pain*? What is this *need* in the sound? Forever unfulfillable yet fulfilling him who hears it, utterly. Is it *Your* need? Can it be Yours? ...'

[*Pause.*]

Dimly the music sounded from the salon above. Dimly the stars shone on the empty street I was suddenly frightened. It seemed to me I had heard a voice of God – and that it issued from a creature whose own voice I had also heard – and it was the voice of an obscene child!

[*Light change. The street scene fades.*]

＊　　＊　　＊

SALIERI'S APARTMENTS.

[*It remains dark.*]

SALIERI: I ran home and buried my fear in work. More pupils – till there were thirty and forty. More committees to help musicians! More motets and anthems to God's glory. And at night I prayed for just one thing. [*He kneels desperately.*] 'Let your voice enter *me*! Let *me* conduct you! ... *Let* me!' [*Pause. He rises.*] As for Mozart, I avoided meeting him – and sent out my Little Winds for whatever scores of his could be found.

[*The VENTICELLI come in with manuscripts. SALIERI sits at the*

fortepiano, and they show him the music alternately, as SERVANTS
unobtrusively remove the Waldstädten table and wing-chair.]

VENTICELLO 1: Six fortepiano sonatas composed in Munich.

VENTICELLO 2: Two in Mannheim.

VENTICELLO 1: A Parisian Symphony.

SALIERI [*to audience*]: Clever. They were all clever. And yet they
seemed to me completely empty!

VENTICELLO 1: A Divertimento in D.

VENTICELLO 2: A Cassazione in G.

VENTICELLO 1: A Grand Litany in E Flat.

SALIERI [*to audience*]: The same. Conventional. Even boring. The
productions of a precocious youngster – Leopold Mozart's swanky
son – nothing more. That Serenade was obviously an exception
in his work: the sort of accident which might visit any composer
on a lucky day!

[*The* VENTICELLI *go off with the music.*]

Had I in fact been simply taken by surprise that the filthy creature
could write music at all? ... Suddenly I felt immensely cheered!
I would seek him out and welcome him myself to Vienna!

*   *   *

THE PALACE OF SCHÖNBRUNN

[*Quick light change. The* EMPEROR JOSEPH *is revealed standing in bright
light before the gilded mirrors and the fireplace, attended by* CHAMBERLAIN
VON STRACK. *His Majesty is a dapper, cheerful figure, aged forty, largely
pleased with himself and the world. Downstage, from opposite sides,* VAN
SWIETEN *and* ORSINI-ROSENBERG *hurry on.*]

JOSEPH: Fêtes and fireworks, gentlemen! Mozart is here! He's waiting
below!

[*All bow.*]

ALL: Majesty!

JOSEPH: *Je suis follement impatient!*

SALIERI [*to audience*]: The Emperor Joseph the Second of Austria. Son of Maria Theresa. Brother of Marie Antoinette. Adorer of music – provided that it made no demands upon the royal brain. [*To the* EMPEROR, *deferentially*] Majesty, I have written a little march in Mozart's honour. May I play it as he comes in?

JOSEPH: By all means, Court Composer. What a delightful idea! Have you met him yet?

SALIERI: Not yet, Majesty.

JOSEPH: Fêtes and fireworks, what fun! Strack, bring him up at once.
[VON STRACK *goes off. The* EMPEROR *comes on to the stage proper.*] *Mon Dieu*, I wish we could have a competition! Mozart against some other virtuoso. Two keyboards in contest. Wouldn't that be fun, Baron?

VAN SWIETEN [*stiffly*]: Not to me, Majesty. In my view, musicians are not horses to be run against one another.
[*Slight pause.*]

JOSEPH: Ah. Well – there it is.
[VON STRACK *returns.*]

VON STRACK: Herr Mozart, Majesty.

JOSEPH: Ah! Splendid! ... [*Conspiratorially he signs to* SALIERI, *who moves quickly to the fortepiano.*] Court Composer – *allons!* [*To* VON STRACK] Admit him, please.

[*Instantly* SALIERI *sits at the instrument and strikes up his March on the keyboard. At the same moment* MOZART *struts in, wearing a highly ornate surcoat, with dress-sword.*

The EMPEROR *stands downstage, centre, his back to the audience, and as* MOZART *approaches he signs to him to halt and listen. Bewildered,* MOZART *does so – becoming aware of* SALIERI *playing his March of Welcome. It is an extremely banal piece, vaguely – but only vaguely – reminiscent of another march to become very famous later on. All stand frozen in attitudes of listening, until* SALIERI *comes to a finish. Applause.*]

JOSEPH [*to* SALIERI]: Charming ... *Comme d'habitude!* [*He turns and extends his hand to be kissed.*] Mozart.

[MOZART *approaches and kneels extravagantly.*]

MOZART: Majesty! Your Majesty's humble slave! Let me kiss your royal hand a hundred thousand times!

[*He kisses it greedily, over and over again, until its owner withdraws it in embarrassment.*]

JOSEPH: *Non, non, s'il vous plaît!* A little less enthusiasm, I beg you. Come sir, *levez-vous!* [*He assists* MOZART *to rise.*] You will not recall it, but the last time we met you were also on the floor! My sister remembers it to this day. This young man – all of six years old, mind you – slipped on the floor at Schönbrunn – came a nasty purler on his little head ... Have I told you this before?

ROSENBERG [*hastily*]: No, Majesty!

VON STRACK [*hastily*]: No, Majesty!

SALIERI [*hastily*]: No, Majesty!

JOSEPH: Well, my sister Antoinette runs forward and picks him up herself. And do you know what he does? Jumps right into her arms – hoopla, just like that! – kisses her on both cheeks and says 'Will you marry me: yes or no?'

[*The* COURTIERS *laugh politely.* MOZART *emits his high-pitched giggle. The* EMPEROR *is clearly startled by it.*]

JOSEPH: I do not mean to embarrass you, Herr Mozart. You know everyone here, surely?

MOZART: Yes, sire. [*Bowing elaborately to* ORSINI-ROSENBERG] Herr Director! [*To* VAN SWIETEN] Herr Prefect.

VAN SWIETEN [*warmly*]: Delighted to see you again.

JOSEPH: But not, I think, our esteemed Court Composer! ... A most serious omission! No one who cares for art can afford not to know Herr Salieri. He wrote that exquisite little March of Welcome for you.

SALIERI: It was a trifle, Majesty.

JOSEPH: Nevertheless ...

MOZART [*to* SALIERI]: I'm overwhelmed, Signore!

JOSEPH: Ideas simply pour out of him – don't they, Strack?

STRACK: Endlessly, sire. [*As if tipping him*] Well done, Salieri.

JOSEPH: Let it be my pleasure then to introduce you! Court Composer Salieri – Herr Mozart of Salzburg!

SALIERI [*sleekly, to* MOZART]: *Finalmente. Che gioia. Che diletto straordinario.*

[*He gives him a prim bow and presents the copy of his music to the other composer, who accepts it with a flood of Italian.*]

MOZART: *Grazie Signore! Mille milione di benvenuti! Sono commosso! È un onore eccezionale incontrarla! Compositore brillante e famosissimo!* [*He makes an elaborate and showy bow in return.*]

SALIERI [*dryly*]: *Grazie.*

JOSEPH: Tell me, Mozart, have you received our commission for the opera?

MOZART: Indeed I have, Majesty! I am so grateful I can hardly speak! ... I swear to you that you will have the best – the most perfect entertainment ever offered a monarch. I've already found a libretto.

ROSENBERG [*startled*]: Have you? I didn't hear of this!

MOZART: Forgive me, Herr Director, I entirely omitted to tell you.

ROSENBERG: May I ask why?

MOZART: It didn't seem very important.

ROSENBERG: Not important?

MOZART: Not really, no.

ROSENBERG [*irritated*]: It is important to *me*, Herr Mozart.

MOZART [*embarrassed*]: Yes, I see that. Of course.

ROSENBERG: And who, pray, is it by?

MOZART: Stephanie.

ROSENBERG: A most unpleasant man.

MOZART: But a brilliant writer.

ROSENBERG: Do you think?

MOZART: The story is really amusing, Majesty. The whole plot is set in a – [*He giggles*] – in a ...

JOSEPH [*eagerly*]: Where? Where is it set?

MOZART: It's – it's – rather saucy, Majesty!

JOSEPH: Yes, yes! Where?

MOZART: Well it's actually set in a *seraglio*.

JOSEPH: A what?

MOZART: A pasha's harem. [*He giggles wildly.*]

ROSENBERG: And you imagine that is a suitable subject for performance at a National Theatre?

MOZART [*in a panic*]: Yes! No! Yes, I mean yes, yes I do. Why not? It's very funny, it's amusing … on my honour – Majesty – there's nothing offensive in it. Nothing offensive in the world. It's full of proper German virtues, I swear it! …

SALIERI [*blandly*]: Scusate, Signore, but what are those? Being a foreigner I'm not sure.

JOSEPH: You are being *cattivo*, Court Composer.

SALIERI: Not at all, Majesty.

JOSEPH: Come then, Mozart. Name us a proper German virtue!

MOZART: Love, Sire. I have yet to see that expressed in any opera.

VAN SWIETEN: Well answered, Mozart.

SALIERI [*smiling*]: Scusate. I was under the impression one rarely saw anything *else* expressed in opera.

MOZART: I mean manly love, Signore. Not male sopranos screeching. Or stupid couples rolling their eyes. All that absurd Italian rubbish.

  [*Pause. Tension.* ORSINI-ROSENBERG *coughs.*]

I mean the real thing.

JOSEPH: And do you know the real thing yourself, Herr Mozart?

MOZART: Under your pardon, I think I do, Majesty. [*He gives a short giggle.*]

JOSEPH: Bravo. When do you think it will be done?

MOZART: The first act is already finished.

JOSEPH: But it can't be more than two weeks since you started!

MOZART: Composing is not hard when you have the right audience to please, Sire.

VAN SWIETEN: A charming reply, Majesty.

JOSEPH: Indeed, Baron. Fêtes and fireworks! I see we are going to have fêtes and fireworks! *Au revoir, Monsieur Mozart. Soyez bienvenu à la cour.*

MOZART [*with expert rapidity*]: *Majesté! — je suis comblé d'honneur d'être accepté dans la maison du Père de tous les musiciens! Servir un monarque aussi plein de discernement que votre Majesté, c'est un honneur qui dépasse le sommet de mes dûs!*

[*A pause. The* EMPEROR *is taken aback by this flood of French.*]

JOSEPH: Ah. Well — there it is. I'll leave you gentlemen to get better acquainted.

SALIERI: Good day, Majesty.

MOZART: *Votre Majesté.*

[*They both bow.* JOSEPH *goes out.*]

ROSENBERG: Good day to you.

VON STRACK: Good day.

[*They follow the* EMPEROR.]

VAN SWIETEN [*warmly shaking his hand*]: Welcome, Mozart. I shall see much more of you. Depend on it!

MOZART: Thank you.

[*He bows. The* BARON *goes.* MOZART *and* SALIERI *are left alone.*]

SALIERI: *Bene.*

MOZART: *Bene.*

SALIERI: I too wish you success with your opera.

MOZART: I'll have it. It's going to be superb. I must tell you I have already found the most excellent singer for the leading part.

SALIERI: Oh: who is that?

MOZART: Her name is Cavalieri. Katherina Cavalieri. She's really German, but she thinks it will advance her career if she sports an Italian name.

SALIERI: She's quite right. It was my idea. She is in fact my prize pupil. Actually she's a very innocent child. Silly in the way of young singers — but, you know, she's only twenty.

[*Without emphasis* MOZART *freezes his movements and* SALIERI *takes one easy step forward to make a fluent aside.*]

[*To audience*] I had kept my hands off Katherina. Yes! But, I could not bear to think of anyone else's upon her — least of all his!

MOZART [*unfreezing*]: You're a good fellow, Salieri! And that's a jolly little thing you wrote for me.

33

SALIERI: It was my pleasure.

MOZART: Let's see if I can remember it. May I?

SALIERI: By all means. It's yours.

MOZART: *Grazie*, Signore.

[MOZART *tosses the manuscript on to the lid of the fortepiano where he cannot see it, sits at the instrument, and plays* SALIERI's *March of Welcome perfectly from memory — at first slowly, recalling it — but on the reprise of the tune, very much faster.*]

The rest is just the same, isn't it?

[*He finishes it with insolent speed.*]

SALIERI: You have a remarkable memory.

MOZART [*delighted with himself*]: *Grazie ancora*, Signore!

[*He plays the opening seven bars again, but this time stops on the interval of the Fourth, and sounds it again with displeasure.*]

It doesn't really *work*, that Fourth — does it! ... Let's try the Third above ... [*He does so — and smiles happily.*] Ah yes! ... Good! ...

[*He repeats the new interval, leading up to it smartly with the well-known military-trumpet arpeggio which characterizes the celebrated March from* The Marriage of Figaro, '*Non più andrai*'. *Then, using the interval — tentatively — delicately — one note at a time, in the treble — he steals into the famous tune itself.*

On and on he plays, improvising happily what is virtually the march we know now, laughing gleefully each time he comes to the amended interval of a Third. SALIERI *watches him with an answering smile painted on his face.*

MOZART's *playing grows more and more exhibitionistic — revealing to the audience the formidable virtuoso he is. The whole time he himself remains totally oblivious to the offence he is giving. Finally he finishes the March with a series of triumphant flourishes and chords!*

An ominous pause.]

SALIERI: *Scusate*. I must go.

MOZART: Really? [*Springing up and indicating the keyboard*] Why don't *you* try a Variation?

SALIERI: Thank you, but I must attend on the Emperor.

MOZART: Ah.

SALIERI: It has been delightful to meet you.

MOZART: For me too! ... And thanks for the March!

[MOZART *picks up the manuscript from the top of the fortepiano and marches happily offstage.*
A slight pause.
SALIERI *moves towards the audience. The lights go down around him.*]

SALIERI [*to audience*]: Was it then – so early – that I began to have thoughts of murder? ... Of course not: at least not in Life. In Art it was a different matter. I decided I would compose a huge tragic opera: something to astonish the world! – and I knew my theme. I would set the Legend of Danaius, who for a monstrous crime was chained to a rock for eternity – his head repeatedly struck by lightning! Wickedly in my head I saw Mozart in that position. In reality the man was in no danger at all ... Not yet.

*   *   *

THE FIRST PERFORMANCE OF
The Abduction from the Seraglio

[*The light changes, and the stage instantly turns into an eighteenth-century theatre. The backdrop projection shows a line of softly gleaming chandeliers.*
The SERVANTS *bring in chairs and benches. Upon them, facing the audience and regarding it as if watching an opera, sit the* EMPEROR JOSEPH, VON STRACK, ORSINI-ROSENBERG *and* VAN SWIETEN.
Next to them: KAPELLMEISTER BONNO *and* TERESA SALIERI.
A little behind them: CONSTANZE. *Behind her:* CITIZENS OF VIENNA.]

SALIERI: The first performance of *The Abduction from the Seraglio*. The creature's expression of manly love.

[MOZART *comes on briskly, wearing a gaudy new coat and a new powdered wig. He struts quickly to the fortepiano, sits at it and mimes conducting.* SALIERI *sits nearby, next to his wife, and watches* MOZART *intently.*]

He himself contrived to wear for the occasion an even more vulgar coat than usual. As for the music, it matched the coat completely. For my dear pupil Katherina Cavalieri he had written quite simply the showiest aria I'd ever heard.

[*Faintly we hear the whizzing scale passages for* SOPRANO *which end the aria 'Marten Aller Arten'.*]

Ten minutes of scales and ornaments, amounting in sum to a vast emptiness. So ridiculous was the piece in fact – so much what might be demanded by a foolish young soprano – that I knew precisely what Mozart must have demanded in return for it.

[*The final orchestral chords of the aria. Silence. No one moves.*]

Although engaged to be married, *he'd had her!* I knew that beyond any doubt. [*Bluntly*] The creature had had my darling girl.

[*Loudly we hear the brilliant Turkish Finale of* Seraglio. *Great applause from those watching.* MOZART *jumps to his feet and acknowledges it. The* EMPEROR *rises – as do all – and gestures graciously to the 'stage' in invitation.* KATHERINA CAVALIERI *runs on in her costume, all plumes and flounces, to renewed cheering and clapping. She curtsies to the* EMPEROR – *is kissed by* SALIERI – *presented to his wife – curtsies again to* MOZART *and, flushed with triumph, moves to one side.*

In the ensuing brief silence CONSTANZE *rushes down from the back, wildly excited. She flings herself on* MOZART, *not even noticing the* EMPEROR.]

CONSTANZE: Oh, well done, lovey! ... Well done, pussy-wussy! ...

[MOZART *indicates the proximity of His Majesty.*]

Oh! ... 'Scuse me! [*She curtsies in embarrassment.*]

MOZART: Majesty, may I present my fiancée, Fraulein Weber.

JOSEPH: *Enchanté, Fraulein.*

CONSTANZE: Your Majesty!

MOZART: Constanze is a singer herself.

JOSEPH: Indeed?

CONSTANZE [*embarrassed*]: I'm not at all, Majesty. Don't be silly, Wolfgang!

JOSEPH: So, Mozart – a good effort. Decidedly that. A good effort.

MOZART: Did you really like it, Sire?

JOSEPH: I thought it was most interesting. Yes, indeed. A trifle – how shall one say? [*To* ORSINI-ROSENBERG] How shall one say, Director?

ROSENBERG [*subserviently*]: Too many notes, Your Majesty?

JOSEPH: Very well put. Too many notes.

MOZART: I don't understand.

JOSEPH: My dear fellow, don't take it too hard. There are in fact only so many notes the ear can hear in the course of an evening. I think I'm right in saying that, aren't I, Court Composer?

SALIERI [*uncomfortably*]: Well yes, I would say yes, on the whole, yes, Majesty.

JOSEPH: There you are. It's clever. It's German. It's quality work. And there are simply too many notes. Do you see?

MOZART: There are just as many notes, Majesty, neither more nor less, as are required.

[*Pause.*]

JOSEPH: Ah ... Well, there it is. [*He goes off abruptly, followed by* ROSENBERG *and* VON STRACK.]

MOZART [*nervous*]: Is he angry?

SALIERI: Not at all. He respects you for your views.

MOZART [*nervously*]: I hope so ... What did you think yourself, sir? Did you care for the piece at all?

SALIERI: Yes, of course, Mozart – at its best it is truly charming.

MOZART: And at other times?

SALIERI [*smoothly*]: Well, just occasionally at other times – in Katherina's aria, for example – it was a little excessive.

MOZART: Katherina is an excessive girl. In fact she's insatiable.

SALIERI: All the same, as my revered teacher the Chevalier Gluck used to say to me – one must avoid music that smells of music.

MOZART: What does that mean?

SALIERI: Music which makes one aware too much of the virtuosity of the composer.

MOZART: Gluck is absurd.

SALIERI: What do you say?

MOZART: He's talked all his life about modernizing opera, but creates people so lofty they sound as though they shit marble.

[CONSTANZE *gives a little scream of shock.*]

CONSTANZE: Oh, 'scuse me! ...

MOZART [*breaking out*]: No, but it's too much! Gluck says! Gluck says! Chevalier Gluck! ... What's Chevalier? I'm a Chevalier. The Pope made me a Chevalier when I was still wetting my bed.

CONSTANZE: Wolferl!

MOZART: Anyway it's ridiculous. Only stupid farts sport titles.

SALIERI [*blandly*]: Such as Court Composer?

MOZART: What? ... [*Realizing*] Ah. Oh. Ha. Ha. Well! ... My father's right again. He always tells me I should padlock my mouth ... Actually, I shouldn't speak at all!

SALIERI [*soothingly*]: Nonsense. I'm just being what the Emperor would call *cattivo*. Won't you introduce me to your charming fiancée?

MOZART: Oh, of course! Constanze, this is Herr Salieri, the Court Composer. Fraulein Weber.

SALIERI [*bowing*]: Delighted, *cara Fraulein*.

CONSTANZE [*bobbing*]: How do you do, Excellency?

SALIERI: May I ask when you marry?

MOZART [*nervously*]: We have to secure my father's consent. He's an excellent man – a wonderful man – but in some ways a little stubborn.

SALIERI: Excuse me, but how old are you?

MOZART: Twenty-six.

SALIERI: Then your father's consent is scarcely indispensable.

CONSTANZE [*to* MOZART]: You see?

MOZART [*uncomfortably*]: Well no, it's not *indispensable* – of course not! ...

SALIERI: My advice to you is to marry and be happy. You have found – it's quite obvious – *un tesoro raro!*

CONSTANZE: Ta very much.

[SALIERI *kisses* CONSTANZE's *hand. She is delighted.*]

SALIERI: Good night to you both.

CONSTANZE: Good night, Excellency!

MOZART: Good night, sir. And thank you … Come, Stanzerl.

[*They depart delightedly. He watches them go.*]

SALIERI [*to audience*]: As I watched her walk away on the arm of the Creature, I felt the lightning thought strike – 'Have her! Her for Katherina!' … Abomination! … Never in my life had I entertained a notion so sinful!

[*Light change: the eighteenth century fades.*]

[*The* VENTICELLI *come on merrily, as if from some celebration. One holds a bottle; the other a glass.*]

VENTICELLO 1: They're married.

SALIERI [*to them*]: What?

VENTICELLO 2: Mozart and Weber – married!

SALIERI: Really?

VENTICELLO 1: His father will be furious!

VENTICELLO 2: They didn't even wait for his consent!

SALIERI: Have they set up house?

VENTICELLO 1: Wipplingerstrasse.

VENTICELLO 2: Number twelve.

VENTICELLO 1: Not bad.

VENTICELLO 2: Considering they've no money.

SALIERI: Is that really true?

VENTICELLO 1: He's wildly extravagant.

VENTICELLO 2: Lives way beyond his means.

SALIERI: But he has pupils.

VENTICELLO 1: Only three.

SALIERI [*to them*]: Why so few?

VENTICELLO 1: He's embarrassing.

VENTICELLO 2: Makes scenes.

VENTICELLO 1: Makes enemies.
VENTICELLO 2: Even Strack, whom he cultivates.
SALIERI: Chamberlain Strack?
VENTICELLO 1: Only last night.
VENTICELLO 2: At Kapellmeister Bonno's.

*   *   *

BONNO'S HOUSE

[*Instant light change.* MOZART *comes in with* VON STRACK. *He is high on wine, and holding a glass. The* VENTICELLI *join the scene, but still talk out of it to Salieri. One of them fills* MOZART's *glass.*]

MOZART: Seven months in this city and not one job! I'm not to be tried again, is that it?
VON STRACK: Of course not.
MOZART: I know what goes on – and so do you. Germany is completely in the hands of foreigners. Worthless wops like *Kapellmeister Bonno!*
VON STRACK: Please! You're in the man's house!
MOZART: Court Composer *Salieri!*
VON STRACK: Hush!
MOZART: Did you see his last opera? – *The Chimney Sweep?* ... Did you?
VON STRACK: Of course I did.
MOZART: Dogshit. Dried dogshit.
VON STRACK [*outraged*]: I beg your pardon!
MOZART [*singing*]: Pom-pom, pom-pom, pom-pom, pom-pom! Tonic and dominant, tonic and dominant from here to resurrection! Not one interesting modulation all night. Salieri is a musical idiot!
VON STRACK: Please!
VENTICELLO 1 [*to* SALIERI]: He'd had too much to drink.
VENTICELLO 2: He often has.

MOZART: Why are Italians so terrified by the slightest complexity in music? Show them one chromatic passage and they *faint!* ... 'Oh how sick!' 'How morbid!' *[Falsetto] Morboso!* ... *Nervoso!* ... *Ohimè!* ... No wonder the music at this court is so dreary.

VON STRACK: Lower your voice.

MOZART: Lower your breeches! . . That's just a joke – just a joke!
[*Unobserved by him* COUNT ORSINI-ROSENBERG *has entered upstage and is suddenly standing between the* VENTICELLI, *listening. He wears a waistcoat of bright green silk, and an expression of supercilious interest.* MOZART *sees him. A pause.*]
[*Pleasantly, to* ORSINI-ROSENBERG] You look like a toad ... I mean you're goggling like a toad. [*He giggles.*]

ROSENBERG [*blandly*]: You would do best to retire tonight, for your own sake.

MOZART: Salieri has fifty pupils. I have three. How am I to live? I'm a married man now! ... Of course I realize you don't concern yourselves with *money* in these exalted circles. All the same, did you know behind his back His Majesty is known as Kaiser Keep It? [*He giggles wildly.*]

VON STRACK: *Mozart!*
[*He stops.*]

MOZART: I shouldn't have said that, should I? ... Forgive me. It was just a joke. Another joke! ... I can't help myself! ... We're all friends here, aren't we?
[VON STRACK *and* ORSINI-ROSENBERG *glare at him. Then* VON STRACK *leaves abruptly, much offended.*]

MOZART: What's wrong with him?

ROSENBERG: Good night.
[*He turns to go.*]

MOZART: No, no, no – please! [*He grabs the* DIRECTOR's *arm.*] Your hand please, first!
[*Unwillingly* ORSINI-ROSENBERG *gives him his hand.* MOZART *kisses it.*]
[*Humbly*] Give me a Post, sir.

ROSENBERG: That is not in my power, Mozart.

MOZART: The Princess Elizabeth is looking for an Instructor. One word from you could secure it for me.

ROSENBERG: I regret that is solely in the recommendation of Court Composer Salieri. [*He disengages himself.*]

MOZART: Do you know I am better than any musician in Vienna? ... Do you?

[ROSENBERG *leaves.* MOZART *calls after him.*]

Foppy-wops – I'm *sick* of them! ... [*Suddenly he giggles to himself, like a child.*] Foppy-wops! Foppy – poppy – snoppy – toppy – hoppy hoppy–wops! – wops!

[*And hops offstage.*]

SALIERI [*watching him go*]: Barely one month later, that thought of revenge became more than thought.

*　*　*

THE WALDSTÄDTEN LIBRARY

[*Two simultaneous shouts bring up the lights. Against the handsome wallpaper stand three masked figures:* CONSTANZE, *flanked on either side by the* VENTICELLI. *All three are guests at a party, and are playing a game of forfeits.*

Two SERVANTS *stand frozen, holding the large wing-chair between them. Two more* SERVANTS *hold the big table of sweetmeats.*]

VENTICELLO 1: Forfeit! ... Forfeit! ...

VENTICELLO 2: Forfeit, Stanzerl! You've got to forfeit!

CONSTANZE: I won't.

VENTICELLO 1: You have to.

VENTICELLO 2: It's the game.

[*The* SERVANTS *unfreeze and set down the furniture.* SALIERI *moves to the wing-chair and sits.*]

SALIERI [*to audience*]: Once again – believe it or not – I was in the same concealing chair in the Baroness's library – [*taking a cup from the little table*] – and consuming the same delicious dessert.

VENTICELLO I: You lost – now there's the penalty!

SALIERI [*to audience*]: A party celebrating the New Year's Eve. I was on my own – my dear spouse Teresa visiting her parents in Italy.

CONSTANZE: Well, *what*? ... What is it?

[VENTICELLO I *snatches up an old-fashioned round ruler from the fortepiano.*]

VENTICELLO I: I want to measure your calves.

CONSTANZE: Oooo!

VENTICELLO I: Well?

CONSTANZE: Definitely not. You cheeky bugger!

VENTICELLO I: Now come on!

VENTICELLO 2: You've got to let him, Stanzerl. All's fair in love and forfeits.

CONSTANZE: No it isn't – so you can both buzz off!

VENTICELLO I: If you don't let me, you won't be allowed to play again.

CONSTANZE: Well choose something else.

VENTICELLO I: I've chosen that. Now get up on the table. Quick, quick! *Allez-oop!* [*Gleefully he shifts the plates of sweetmeats from the table.*]

CONSTANZE: Quick, then! ... Before anyone sees!

[*The two masked men lift the shrieking masked girl up on to the table.*]

VENTICELLO I: Hold her, Friedrich.

CONSTANZE: I don't have to be held, thank you!

VENTICELLO 2: Yes, you do: that's part of the penalty.

[*He holds her ankles firmly, while* VENTICELLO I *thrusts the ruler under her skirts and measures her legs. Excitedly* SALIERI *reverses his position so that he can kneel in the wing-chair, and watch.* CONSTANZE *giggles delightedly, then becomes outraged – or pretends to be.*]

CONSTANZE: Stop it! ... Stop that! That's quite enough of that!

[*She bends down and tries to slap him.*]

VENTICELLO 1: Seventeen inches – knee to ankle!

VENTICELLO 2: Let me do it! You hold her!

CONSTANZE: That's not fair!

VENTICELLO 2: Yes, it is. You lost to me too.

CONSTANZE: It's been done now! Let me *down*!

VENTICELLO 2: Hold her, Karl.

CONSTANZE: No! ...

> [VENTICELLO 1 *holds her ankles.* VENTICELLO 2 *thrusts his head entirely under her skirts. She squeals.*]

No – stop it! ... No! ...

> [*In the middle of this undignified scene* MOZART *comes rushing on – also masked.*]

MOZART [*outraged*]: Constanze!

> [*They freeze.* SALIERI *ducks back down and sits hidden in the chair.*]

Gentlemen, if you please.

CONSTANZE: It's only a game, Wolferl! ...

VENTICELLO 1: We meant no harm, 'pon my word.

MOZART [*stiffly*]: Come down off that table please.

> [*They hand her down.*]

Thank you. We'll see you later.

VENTICELLO 2: Now look, Mozart, don't be pompous –

MOZART: Please excuse us now.

> [*They go. The little man is very angry. He tears off his mask.*]

[*To* CONSTANZE] Do you realize what you've done?

CONSTANZE: No, what? ... [*Flustered, she busies herself restoring the plates of sweetmeats to the table.*]

MOZART: Just lost your reputation, that's all! You're now a loose girl.

CONSTANZE: Don't be so stupid. [*She too removes her mask.*]

MOZART: You are a married woman, for God's sake!

CONSTANZE: And what of it?

MOZART: A young wife does not allow her legs to be handled in public. Couldn't you at least have measured your own ugly legs?

CONSTANZE: *What*?

MOZART [*raising his voice*]: Do you know what you've done?! ...
You've shamed me – that's all! *Shamed* me!

CONSTANZE: Oh, don't be so ridiculous!

MOZART: Shamed me – in front of *them*!

CONSTANZE [*suddenly furious*]: *You?* Shamed *you?* ... That's a laugh!
If there's any shame around, lovey, it's *mine*!

MOZART: What do you mean?

CONSTANZE: You've only had every pupil who ever came to you.

MOZART: That's not true.

CONSTANZE: Every single female pupil!

MOZART: Name them! *Name them!*

CONSTANZE: The Aurnhammer girl! The Rumbeck girl! Katherina Cavalieri – that sly little whore! *She* wasn't even your
pupil – she was Salieri's. Which actually, my dear, may be why
he has hundreds and you have none! He doesn't drag them into
bed!

MOZART: Of course he doesn't! He can't get it up, that's why! ...
Have you heard his music? That's the sound of someone who
can't get it up! At least *I* can do that!

CONSTANZE: I'm sick of you!

MOZART [*shouting*]: No one ever said I couldn't do *that*!

CONSTANZE [*bursting into tears*]: I don't give a fart! I hate you!
I hate you for ever and ever – I hate you! [*A tiny pause. She
weeps.*]

MOZART [*helplessly*]: Oh Stanzerl, don't cry. Please don't cry ...
I can't bear it when you cry. I just didn't want you to look cheap
in people's eyes, that's all. Here! [*He snatches up the ruler.*] Beat
me ... Beat me ... I'm your slave. Stanzi marini. Stanzi marini bini
gini. I'll just stand here like a little lamb and bear your strokes.
Here. Do it ... *Batti.*

CONSTANZE: No.

MOZART: *Batti, batti. Mio tesoro!*

CONSTANZE: No!

MOZART: Stanzerly wanzerly piggly poo!

CONSTANZE: Stop it.

MOZART: Stanzy wanzy had a fit! Shit her stays and made them split!

[*She giggles despite herself.*]

CONSTANZE: Stop it!

MOZART: When they took away her skirt, Stanzy wanzy ate the dirt!

CONSTANZE: Stop it now! [*She snatches the ruler and gives him a whack with it. He yowls playfully.*]

MOZART: Oooo! Oooo! Oooo! Do it again! Do it again! I cast myself at your stinking feet, Madonna!

[*He does so. She whacks him some more as he crouches, but always lightly, scarcely looking at him, divided between tears and laughter.* MOZART *drums his feet with pleasure.*]

MOZART: Ow! Ow! Ow!

[*And then suddenly* SALIERI, *unable to bear another second, cries out involuntarily.*]

SALIERI: *Ah!!!*

[*The young couple freeze.* SALIERI – *discovered* – *hastily converts his noise of disgust into a yawn, and stretches as if waking up from a nap. He peers out of the wing-chair.*]

SALIERI: Good evening.

CONSTANZE [*embarrassed*]: Excellency ...

MOZART: How long have you been there?

SALIERI: I was asleep until a second ago. Are you two quarrelling?

MOZART: No, of course not.

CONSTANZE: Yes, we are. He's being very irritating.

SALIERI [*rising*]: *Caro Herr*, tonight is the time for New Year resolutions. Irritating lovely ladies cannot surely be one of yours. May I suggest you bring us each a *sorbetto* from the dining-room?

MOZART: But why don't we all go to the table?

CONSTANZE: Herr Salieri is quite right. Bring them here – it'll be your punishment.

MOZART: Stanzi!

SALIERI: Come now, I can keep your wife company. There cannot be a better peace offering than a *sorbetto* of aniseed.

CONSTANZE: I prefer tangerine.

SALIERI: Very well, tangerine. [*Greedily*] But if you could possibly manage aniseed for me, I'd be deeply obliged ... So the New Year can begin coolly for all three of us.

[*A pause.* MOZART *hesitates – and then bows.*]

MOZART: I'm honoured, Signore, of course. And then I'll play you at billiards. What do you say?

SALIERI: I'm afraid I don't play.

MOZART [*with surprise*]: You don't?

CONSTANZE: Wolferl would rather play at billiards than anything. He's very good at it.

MOZART: I'm the best! I may nod occasionally at composing, but at billiards – never!

SALIERI: A virtuoso of the cue.

MOZART: Exactly! It's a virtuoso's game! ... [*He snatches up the ruler and treats it as if it were a cue.*] I think I shall write a Grand Fantasia for Billiard Balls! Trillos! Acciaccaturas! Whole arpeggios in ivory! Then I'll play it myself in public! ... It'll have to be *me* because none of those Italian charlatans like Clementi will be able to get his fingers round the cue! *Scusate*, Signore!

[*He gives a swanky flourish of the hand and struts off.*]

CONSTANZE: He's a love, really.

SALIERI: And lucky, too, in you. You are, if I may say so, an astonishing creature.

CONSTANZE: Me? ... Ta very much.

SALIERI: On the other hand, your husband does not appear to be so thriving.

CONSTANZE [*seizing her opportunity*]: We're desperate, sir.

SALIERI: What?

CONSTANZE: We've no money and no prospects of any. That's the truth.

SALIERI: I don't understand. He gives many public concerts.

CONSTANZE: They don't pay enough. What he needs is pupils. Illustrious pupils. His father calls us spendthrifts, but that's unfair. I manage as well as anyone could. There's simply not enough. Don't tell him I talked to you, please.

SALIERI [*intimately*]: This is solely between us. How can I help?

CONSTANZE: My husband needs security, sir. If only he could find regular employment, everything would be all right. Is there nothing at Court?

SALIERI: Not at the moment.

CONSTANZE [*harder*]: The Princess Elizabeth needs a tutor.

SALIERI: Really? I hadn't heard.

CONSTANZE: One word from you and the post would be his. Other pupils would follow at once ...

SALIERI [*looking off*]: He's coming back.

CONSTANZE: Please ... please, Excellency. You can't imagine what a difference it would make.

SALIERI: We can't speak of it now.

CONSTANZE: When then? Oh, please!

SALIERI: Can you come and see me tomorrow? Alone?

CONSTANZE: I can't do that.

SALIERI: I'm a married man.

CONSTANZE: All the same.

SALIERI: When does he work?

CONSTANZE: Afternoons.

SALIERI: Then come at three.

CONSTANZE: I can't possibly!

SALIERI: Yes or no? In his interests?

[*A pause. She hesitates – opens her mouth – then smiles and abruptly runs off.*]

SALIERI [*to audience*]: So I'd done it! Spoken aloud. Invited her! What of that vow made in church? Fidelity – virtue – all of that? I couldn't think of that now! ...

[SERVANTS *remove the Waldstädten furniture. Others replace it with two small gilded chairs, centre, quite close together. Others again surreptitiously bring in the old dressing-gown and shawl which Salieri discarded before Scene Three, placing them on the fortepiano.*]

* * *

SALIERI'S SALON

[*On the curtains are thrown again projections of long windows.*]

SALIERI: Next afternoon I waited in a fever! Would she come? I had no idea. And if she did, how would I behave? I had no idea of that either. Was I actually going to seduce a young wife of two months' standing? ... Part of me – much of me – wanted it, badly. *Badly.* Yes, badly was the word! ...

[*The clock strikes three. On the first stroke the bell sounds. He rises excitedly.*]

There she was! On the stroke! She'd come ... She'd *come!*

[*Enter from the right the* COOK, *still as fat, but forty years younger. He proudly carries a plate piled with brandied chestnuts.* SALIERI *takes them from him nervously, nodding with approval, and sets them on the table.*]

[*To the* COOK] *Grazie. Grazie tanti ... Via, via, via!*

[*The* COOK *bows as* SALIERI *dismisses him, and goes out the same way, smirking suggestively. The* VALET *comes in from the left – he is also forty years younger – and behind him* CONSTANZE, *wearing a pretty hat and carrying a portfolio.*]

SALIERI: Signora!

CONSTANZE [*curtseying*]: Excellency.

SALIERI: *Benvenuta.* [*To* VALET *in dismissal*] *Grazie.*

[*The* VALET *goes.*]

Well. You have come.

CONSTANZE: I should not have done. My husband would be frantic if he knew. He's a very jealous man

SALIERI: Are you a jealous woman?

CONSTANZE: Why do you ask?

SALIERI: It's not a passion I understand ... You're looking even prettier than you were last night, if I may say so.

CONSTANZE: Ta very much! ... I brought you some manuscripts by Wolfgang. When you see them you'll understand how right he is for a royal appointment. Will you look at them, please, while I wait?

SALIERI: You mean now?

CONSTANZE: Yes, I have to take them back with me. He'll miss them otherwise. He doesn't make copies. These are all the originals.

SALIERI: Sit down. Let me offer you something special.

CONSTANZE [sitting]: What's that?

SALIERI [producing the box]: Capezzoli di Venere. Nipples of Venus. Roman chestnuts in brandied sugar.

CONSTANZE: No, thank you.

SALIERI: Do try. My cook made them especially for you.

CONSTANZE: Me?

SALIERI: Yes. They're quite rare.

CONSTANZE: Well then, I'd better, hadn't I? Just one ... Ta very much. [She takes one and puts it in her mouth. The taste amazes her.] Oh! ... Oh! ... Oh! ... They're delish!

SALIERI [lustfully watching her eat]: Aren't they?

CONSTANZE: Mmmmm!

SALIERI: Have another.

CONSTANZE [taking two more]: I couldn't possibly.

[Carefully he moves round behind her, and seats himself on the chair next to her.]

SALIERI: I think you're the most generous girl in the world.

CONSTANZE: Generous?

SALIERI: It's my word for you. I thought last night that Constanze is altogether too stiff a name for that girl. I shall rechristen her 'Generosa'. La Generosa. Then I'll write a glorious song for her under that title and she'll sing it, just for me.

CONSTANZE [*smiling*]: I am much out of practice, sir.

SALIERI: *La Generosa.* [*He leans a little towards her.*] Don't tell me it's going to prove inaccurate, my name for you.

.CONSTANZE [*coolly*]: What name do you give your wife, Excellency?

SALIERI [*equally coolly*]: I'm not an Excellency, and I call my wife Signora Salieri. If I named her anything else it would be *La Statua.* She's a very upright lady.

CONSTANZE: Is she here now? I'd like to meet her.

SALIERI: Alas, no. At the moment she's visiting her mother in Verona.

[*She starts very slightly out of her chair.* SALIERI *gently restrains her.*]

Constanze: tomorrow evening I dine with the Emperor. One word from me recommending your husband as Tutor to the Princess Elizabeth, and that invaluable post is his. Believe me, when I speak to His Majesty in matters musical, no one contradicts me.

CONSTANZE: I believe you.

SALIERI: *Bene.* [*Still sitting, he takes his mouchoir and delicately wipes her mouth with it.*] Surely service of that sort deserves a little recompense in return?

CONSTANZE: How little?

[*Slight pause.*]

SALIERI: The size of a kiss.

[*Slight pause.*]

CONSTANZE: Just one?

[*Slight pause.*]

SALIERI: If one seems fair to you.

[*She looks at him — then kisses him lightly on the mouth.*
Longer pause.]

Does it?

[*She gives him a longer kiss. He makes to touch her with his hand.*
She breaks off.]

CONSTANZE: I fancy that's fairness enough.

[*Pause.*]

SALIERI [*carefully*]: A pity ... It's somewhat small pay, to secure a post every musician in Vienna is hoping for.

CONSTANZE: What do you mean?

SALIERI: Is it not clear?

CONSTANZE: No. Not at all.

SALIERI: Another pity ... A thousand pities.

[*Pause.*]

CONSTANZE: I don't believe it ... I just don't believe it!

SALIERI: What?

CONSTANZE: What you've just said.

SALIERI [*hastily*]: I said nothing. What did I say?

[CONSTANZE *gets up and* SALIERI *rises in panic.*]

CONSTANZE: Oh, I'm going! ... I'm getting out of this!

SALIERI: Constanze ...

CONSTANZE: Let me pass, please.

SALIERI: Constanze, listen to me! I'm a clumsy man. You think me sophisticated – I'm not at all. Take a true look. I've no cunning. I live on ink and sweetmeats. I never see women at all ... When I met you last night, I envied Mozart from the depths of my soul. Out of that envy came stupid thoughts. For one silly second I dared imagine that – out of the vast store you obviously possess – you might spare me one coin of tenderness your rich husband does not need – and inspire me also.

[*Pause. She laughs.*]

I amuse.

CONSTANZE: Mozart was right. You're wicked.

SALIERI: He said that?

CONSTANZE: 'All wops are performers,' he said. 'Be very careful with that one.' Meaning you. He was being comic of course.

SALIERI: Yes.

[*Abruptly he turns his back on her.*]

CONSTANZE: But not that comic, actually. I mean you're acting a pretty obvious role, aren't you, dear? A small town boy, and all the time as clever as cutlets! ... [*Mock tender*] Ah! – are you sulking? *Are* you? ... When Mozart sulks I smack his botty. He rather likes it. Do you want me to scold you a bit and smack your botty too? [*She hits him lightly with the portfolio. He turns in a fury.*]

SALIERI: How dare you?! ... *You silly, common girl!*

[*A dreadful silence.*]

[*Icy*] Forgive me. Let us confine our talk to your husband. He is a brilliant keyboard player, no question. However, the Princess Elizabeth also requires a tutor in vocal music. I am not convinced he is the man for that. I would like to look at the pieces you've brought, and decide if he is mature enough. I will study them overnight – and you will study my proposal. Not to be vague: that is the price. [*He extends his hand for the portfolio, and she surrenders it.*] Good afternoon.

[*He turns from her and places it on a chair. She lingers – tries to speak – cannot – and goes out quickly.*]

*   *   *

THE SAME

[SALIERI *turns in a ferment to the audience.*]

SALIERI: Fiasco! ... Fiasco! ... The sordidness of it! The sheer sweating sordidness! ... Worse than if I'd actually done it! ... To be that much in sin and feel so *ridiculous* as well! ... I didn't deserve any pity from the Old Bargainer above! There was no excuse. If now my music was rejected by Him forever, it was my fault, mine alone. Would she return tomorrow? Never. And if she did, what then? What would I do? [*Brutally*] What would I actually *do*? ... Apologize profoundly – or try again? ... [*Crying out*] *Nobile, nobile Salieri!* ... What had he done to me – this Mozart! Before he came did I behave like this? Did I? Toy with adultery? Blackmail women? It was all going – slipping – growing rotten – because of *him*!

[*He moves upstage in a fever – reaches out to take the portfolio on*

the chair — but as if fearful of what he might find inside it he
withdraws his hand and sits instead. A pause. He contemplates the
music lying there as if it were a great confection he is dying to eat,
but dare not. Then suddenly he snatches at it — tears the ribbon —
opens the case and stares greedily at the manuscripts within.
Music sounds instantly, faintly, in the theatre, as his eye falls on
the first page. It is the opening of the Twenty-ninth Symphony, in
A Major.]

[*Over the music, reading it*] She had said that these were his original
scores. First and only drafts of the music. Yet they looked like fair
copies. They showed no corrections of any kind.

[*He looks up from the manuscript at the audience: the music abruptly*
stops.]

It was puzzling — then suddenly alarming. What was evident was
that Mozart was simply transcribing music —

[*He resumes looking at the music. Immediately the Sinfonia*
Concertante for Violin and Viola sounds faintly.]

— completely finished in his head. And finished as most music
is never finished.

[*He looks up again: the music breaks off.*]

Displace one note and there would be diminishment. Displace one
phrase and the structure would fall.

[*He resumes reading, and the music also resumes: a ravishing phrase*
from the slow movement of the Concerto for Flute and Harp.]

Here again — only now in abundance — were the same sounds
I'd heard in the library. The same crushed harmonies — glancing
collisions — agonizing delights.

[*And he looks up: again the music stops.*]

The truth was clear. That Serenade had been no accident.

[*Very low, in the theatre, a faint thundery sound is heard accumulating,*
like a distant sea.]

I was staring through the cage of those meticulous ink strokes
at an Absolute Beauty!

[*And out of the thundery roar writhes and rises the clear sound of*
a soprano, singing the Kyrie from the C Minor Mass. The accretion

*of noise around her voice falls away — it is suddenly clear and bright
— then clearer and brighter. The light also grows bright: too bright:
burning white, then scalding white!* SALIERI *rises in the downpour
of the music which is growing ever louder — filling the theatre —
as the soprano yields to the full chorus, fortissimo, singing its massive
counterpoint.*

This is by far the loudest sound the audience has yet heard. SALIERI
*staggers towards us, holding the manuscripts in his hand, like a man
caught in a tumbling and violent sea.*

Finally the drums crash in below: SALIERI *drops the portfolio of
manuscripts — and falls senseless to the ground. At the same second
the music explodes into a long, echoing, distorted boom, signifying
some dreadful annihilation.*

*The sound remains suspended over the prone figure in a menacing
continuum — no longer music at all. Then it dies away, and there
is only silence.*

The light fades again.

A long pause.

SALIERI *quite still, his head by the pile of manuscripts.*

Finally the clock sounds: nine times. SALIERI *stirs as it does. Slowly
he raises his head and looks up. And now — quietly at first — he
addresses his God.*]

SALIERI: *Capisco!* I know my fate. Now for the first time I feel
my emptiness as Adam felt his nakedness ... [*Slowly he rises to
his feet.*] Tonight at an inn somewhere in this city stands a giggling
child who can put on paper, without actually setting down his
billiard cue, casual notes which turn my most considered ones into
lifeless scratches. *Grazie*, Signore! You gave me the desire to serve
you — which most men do not have — then saw to it the service was
shameful in the ears of the server. *Grazie!* You gave me the desire
to praise you — which most do not feel — then made me mute.
Grazie tante! You put into me perception of the Incomparable
— which most men never know! — then ensured that I would know
myself forever mediocre. [*His voice gains power.*] Why? ... What
is my fault? ... Until this day I have pursued virtue with rigour.

I have laboured long hours to relieve my fellow men. I have worked and worked the talent you allowed me. [*Calling up*] *You know how hard I've worked!* – solely that in the end, in the practice of the art which alone makes the world comprehensible to me, I might hear Your Voice! And now I do hear it – and it says only one name: MOZART! ... Spiteful, sniggering, conceited, infantine Mozart! – who has never worked one minute to help another man! – shit-talking Mozart with his botty-smacking wife! – *him* you have chosen to be your sole conduct! And *my* only reward – my sublime privilege – is to be the sole man alive in this time who shall clearly recognize your Incarnation! [*Savagely*] *Grazie e grazie ancora!* [*Pause.*] So be it! From this time we are enemies, You and I! I'll not accept it from You – *Do you hear?* ... They say God is not mocked. I tell you, *Man* is not mocked! *I* am not mocked! ... They say the spirit bloweth where it listeth: I tell you NO! It must list to virtue or not blow at all! [*Yelling*] *Dio Ingiusto!* – You are the Enemy! I name Thee now – *Nemico Eterno!* And this I swear. To my last breath I shall *block* you on earth, as far as I am able! [*He glares up at God. To audience*] What use, after all, is Man, if not to teach God His lessons? [*Pause. Suddenly he speaks again to us in the voice of an old man.*] And now –

[*He slips off his powdered wig, crosses to the fortepiano and takes from its lid the old dressing-gown and shawl which he discarded when he conducted us back to the eighteenth century. These he slips on over his court coat. It is again 1823.*]

before I tell you what happened next – God's answer to me – and indeed Constanze's – and all the horrors that followed – let me stop. The bladder, being a human appendage, is not something you need concern yourselves with yet. I being alive, though barely, am at its constant call. It is now one hour before dawn – when I must dismiss us both. When I return I'll tell you about the war I fought with God through his preferred Creature – Mozart, named *Amadeus*. In the waging of which, of course, the Creature had to be destroyed.

[*He bows to the audience with malignant slyness — snatches a pastry from the stand — and leaves the stage, chewing at it voraciously. The manuscripts lie where he spilled them in his fall.*
The lights in the theatre come up as he goes.]

END OF ACT I

ACT 2

[*The lights go down in the theatre as* SALIERI *returns.*]

SALIERI: I have been listening to the cats in the courtyard. They are all singing Rossini. It is obvious that cats have declined as badly as composers. Domenico Scarlatti owned one which would actually stroll across the keyboard and pick out passable subjects for fugue. But that was a Spanish cat of the Enlightenment. It appreciated counterpoint. Nowadays all cats appreciate are High Cs. Like the rest of the public.

[*He comes downstage and addresses the audience directly.*]

This is now the very last hour of my life. You must understand me. Not forgive. I do not seek forgiveness. I was a good man, as the world calls good. What use was it to me? Goodness could not make me a good composer. Was Mozart good? Goodness is nothing in the furnace of art.

[*Pause.*]

On that dreadful Night of the Manuscripts my life acquired a terrible and thrilling purpose. The blocking of God in one of his purest manifestations. I had the power. God needed Mozart to let himself into the world. And Mozart needed me to get him worldly advancement. So it would be a battle to the end – and Mozart was the battleground.

[*Pause.*]

One thing I knew of Him. He was a cunning Enemy. Witness the fact that in blocking Him in the world I was also given the satisfaction of obstructing a disliked human rival. I wonder which of you will refuse that chance if it is offered.

[*He regards the audience maliciously, taking off his dressing gown and shawl.*]

I felt the danger at once, as soon as I'd uttered my challenge. How would He answer? Would He strike me dead for my impiety? Don't laugh. I was not a sophisticate of the salons. I was a small-town Catholic, full of dread!

[*He puts on his powdered wig, and speaks again in his younger voice. We are back in the eighteenth century.*]

The first thing that happened — barely one hour later —

[*The doorbell sounds.* CONSTANZE *comes in followed by a helpless* VALET.]

Suddenly Constanze was back. At ten o'clock at night! [*In surprise*] Signora!

CONSTANZE [*stiffly*]: My husband is at a soirée of Baron van Swieten. A concert of Sebastian Bach. He didn't think I would enjoy it.

SALIERI: I see. [*Curtly, to the goggling* VALET] I'll ring if we require anything. Thank you.

[*The* VALET *goes out. Slight pause.*]

CONSTANZE [*flatly*]: Where do we go, then?

SALIERI: What?

CONSTANZE: Do we do it in here? ... Why not?

[*She sits, still wearing her hat, in one of the little gilded upright chairs.*

Deliberately she loosens the strings of her bodice, so that one can just see the tops of her breasts, hitches up her silk skirts above the knees, so that one can also just see the flesh above the tops of the stockings, spreads her legs and regards him with an open stare.]

[*Speaking softly*] Well? ... Let's get on with it.

[*For a second* SALIERI *returns the stare, then suddenly looks away.*]

SALIERI [*stiffly*]: Your manuscripts are there. Please take them and go. Now. At once.

[*Pause.*]

CONSTANZE: You shit.

[*She jumps up and snatches the portfolio.*]

SALIERI: *Via! Don't return!*

CONSTANZE: You rotten shit!

[*Suddenly she runs at him – trying furiously to hit at his face. He grabs her arms, shakes her violently, and hurls her on the floor.*]

SALIERI: *Via!*

[*She freezes, staring up at him in hate.*]

[*Calling to the audience*] You see how it was! I would have liked her – oh yes, just then more than ever! But now I wanted nothing petty! ... My quarrel wasn't with Mozart – it was *through* him! Through him to God who loved him so. [*Scornfully*] Amadeus! ... Amadeus! ...

[CONSTANZE *picks herself up and runs from the room.*

Pause. He calms himself, going to the table and selecting a 'Nipple of Venus' to eat.]

The next day, when Katherina Cavalieri came for her lesson, I made the same halting speech about 'coins of tenderness' – and I dubbed the girl *La Generosa*. I regret that my invention in love, as in art, has always been limited. Fortunately Katherina found it sufficient. She consumed twenty 'Nipples of Venus' – kissed me with brandied breath – and slipped easily into my bed.

[KATHERINA *comes in languidly, half-undressed, as if from his bedroom. He embraces her, and helps slyly to adjust her peignoir.*]

She remained there as my mistress for many years behind my good wife's back – and I soon erased in sweat the sense of his little body, the Creature's, preceding me.

[KATHERINA *gives him a radiant smile, and ambles off.*]

So much for my vow of sexual virtue. [*Slight pause.*] The same evening I went to the Palace and resigned from all my committees to help the lot of poor musicians. So much for my vow of social virtue.

[*Light change.*]

Then I went to the Emperor and recommended a man of no talent whatever to instruct the Princess Elizabeth.

* * *

THE PALACE OF SCHÖNBRUNN

[*The* EMPEROR *stands before the vast fireplace, between the golden mirrors.*]

JOSEPH: Herr Sommer. A dull man, surely? What of Mozart?

SALIERI: Majesty, I cannot with a clear conscience recommend Mozart to teach Royalty. One hears too many stories.

JOSEPH: They may be just gossip.

SALIERI: One of them I regret relates to a protégé of my own. A very young singer.

JOSEPH: *Charmant!*

SALIERI: Not pleasant, Majesty, but true.

JOSEPH: I see ... Let it be Herr Sommer, then. [*He walks down on to the main stage.*] I daresay he can't do much harm. To be frank, no one can do much harm musically to the Princess Elizabeth. [*He strolls away.*]

> [SALIERI *goes.* MOZART *enters from the other side, downstage. He wears a more natural-looking wig from now on: one indeed intended to represent his own hair of light chestnut, full and gathered at the back with ribbon.*]

SALIERI [*to audience*]: Mozart certainly did not suspect me. The Emperor announced the appointment in his usual way —

JOSEPH [*pausing*]: Well, there it is.

> [JOSEPH *goes off.*]

SALIERI: — and I commiserated with the loser.

> [MOZART *turns and stares bleakly out front.* SALIERI *shakes his hand.*]

MOZART [*bitterly*]: It's my own fault. My father always writes I should be more obedient. *Know my place!* ... He'll send me sixteen lectures when he hears of this!

> [MOZART *goes slowly up to the fortepiano. Lights lower.*]

SALIERI [*to audience, watching him*]: It was a most serious loss as far as Mozart was concerned.

* * *

VIENNA, AND GLIMPSES OF OPERA HOUSES

[*The* VENTICELLI *glide on.*]

VENTICELLO 1: His list of pupils hardly moves.

VENTICELLO 2: Six at most.

VENTICELLO 1: And now a child to keep!

VENTICELLO 2: A boy.

SALIERI: Poor fellow. [*To audience*] I, by contrast, prospered. This is the extraordinary truth. If I had expected anger from God – none came. *None!* ... Instead – incredibly – in eighty-four and eighty-five I came to be regarded as infinitely the superior composer. And this despite the fact that these were the two years in which Mozart wrote his best keyboard concerti and his string quartets.

[*The* VENTICELLI *stand on either side of* SALIERI. MOZART *sits at the fortepiano.*]

VENTICELLO 1: Haydn calls the quartets unsurpassed.

SALIERI: They were – but no one heard them.

VENTICELLO 2: Van Swieten calls the concerti sublime.

SALIERI: They were, but no one noticed.

[MOZART *plays and conducts from the keyboard. Faintly we hear the Rondo from the Piano Concerto in A Major, K.488.*]

[*Over this*] The Viennese greeted each concerto with the squeals of pleasure they usually reserved for a new style of bonnet. Each was played once – then totally forgotten! I alone was empowered to recognize them for what they were: the finest things made by man in the whole of the eighteenth century ... By contrast, my operas were played everywhere and saluted by everyone! I composed my *Semiramide* for Munich.

VENTICELLO 1: Rapturously received!

VENTICELLO 2: People *faint* with pleasure!

[*In the Light Box is seen the interior of a brilliantly coloured Opera House, and an audience standing up applauding vigorously.* SALIERI, *flanked by the* VENTICELLI, *turns upstage and bows to it. The concerto can scarcely be heard through the din.*]

SALIERI: I wrote a comic opera for Vienna. *La Grotta di Trofonio.*

VENTICELLO 1: The talk of the city!

VENTICELLO 2: The cafés are buzzing!

[*Another Opera House interior is lit up. Another audience claps vigorously. Again* SALIERI *bows to it.*]

SALIERI [*to audience*]: I finally finished my tragic opera *Danaius*, and produced it in Paris.

VENTICELLO 1: Stupendous reception!

VENTICELLO 2: The plaudits shake the roof!

VENTICELLO 1: Your name sounds throughout the Empire!

VENTICELLO 2: Throughout all Europe!

[*Yet another Opera House and another excited audience.* SALIERI *bows a third time. Even the* VENTICELLI *now applaud him. The concerto stops.* MOZART *rises from the keyboard and, while* SALIERI *speaks, crosses directly through the scene and leaves the stage.*]

SALIERI [*to audience*]: It was incomprehensible. Almost as if I were being pushed deliberately from triumph to triumph! ... I filled my head with golden opinions – yes, and this house with golden furniture!

✳   ✳   ✳

SALIERI'S SALON

[*The stage turns gold.*
SERVANTS *come on carrying golden chairs upholstered in golden brocade. They place these all over the wooden floor.*
The VALET *appears, a little older, divests* SALIERI *of his sky-blue coat and clothes him instead in a frock-coat of gold satin.*
The COOK *– also of course a little older – brings in a golden cake-stand piled with more elaborate cakes.*]

SALIERI: My own taste was for plain things – but I *denied* it! ... I grew confident. I grew resplendent. I gave salons and soirées, and worshipped the season round at the altar of Success!

[*He sits at ease in his salon. The* VENTICELLI *sit with him, one on either side.*]

VENTICELLO 1: Mozart heard your comedy last night.

VENTICELLO 2: He spoke of it to the Princess Lichnowsky.

VENTICELLO 1: He said you should be made to clean up your own mess.

SALIERI [*taking snuff*]: *Really?* What charmers these Salzburgers are!

VENTICELLO 2: People are outraged by him.

VENTICELLO 1: He empties drawing-rooms. Now Van Swieten is angry with him.

SALIERI: Lord Fugue? I thought he was the Baron's little pet.

VENTICELLO 2: Mozart has asked leave to write an Italian opera.

SALIERI [*briskly aside to audience*]: Italian opera! Threat! My kingdom!

VENTICELLO 1: And the Baron is scandalized.

SALIERI: But why? What's the theme of it?

[VAN SWIETEN *comes on quickly from upstage.*]

VAN SWIETEN: Figaro! ... *The Marriage of Figaro!* That disgraceful play of Beaumarchais!

[*At a discreet sign of dismissal from* SALIERI, *the* VENTICELLI *slip away.* VAN SWIETEN *joins* SALIERI, *and sits on one of the gold chairs.*]

[*To* SALIERI] That's all he can find to waste his talent on: a vulgar farce! Noblemen lusting after chambermaids! Their wives dressing up in stupid disguises anyone could penetrate in a second! ... When I reproved him, he said I reminded him of his father! ... I simply cannot imagine why Mozart should want to set that rubbish!

[MOZART *enters quickly from upstage, accompanied by* VON STRACK. *They join* SALIERI *and* VAN SWIETEN.]

MOZART: Because I want to do a piece about real people, Baron! And I want to set it in a real place! A *boudoir!* – because that to me is the most exciting place on earth! Underclothes on the floor!

Sheets still warm from a woman's body! Even a pisspot brimming under the bed!

VAN SWIETEN [*outraged*]: Mozart!

MOZART: I want life, Baron. Not boring legends!

VON STRACK: Herr Salieri's recent *Danaius* was a legend and that did not bore the French.

MOZART: It is impossible to bore the French – except with real life!

VAN SWIETEN: I had assumed, now that you had joined our Brotherhood of Masons, you would choose more elevated themes.

MOZART [*impatiently*]: Oh elevated! Elevated! ... The only thing a man should elevate is his doodle.

VAN SWIETEN: You are provoking, sir! Has everything to be a joke with you?

MOZART [*desperate*]: Excuse language, Baron, but really! ... How can we go on forever with these gods and heroes?

VAN SWIETEN [*passionately*]: Because they *go* on forever – that's why! They represent the eternal in us. Opera is here to ennoble us, Mozart – you and me just as well as the Emperor. It is an aggrandizing art! It celebrates the eternal in Man and ignores the ephemeral. The goddess in Woman and not the laundress.

VON STRACK: Well said, sir. Exactly!

MOZART [*imitating his drawl*]: Oh well said, yes, well said! Exactly! [*To all of them*] I don't understand you! You're all up on perches, but it doesn't hide your arseholes! You don't give a shit about gods and heroes! If you are honest – each one of you – which of you isn't more at home with his hairdresser than Hercules? Or Horatius? [*To* SALIERI] Or your stupid *Danaius*, come to that! Or mine – mine! – *Idomeneo, King of Crete*! All those anguished antiques! They're all bores! Bores, bores, bores! [*Suddenly he springs up and jumps on to a chair, like an orator. Declaring it*] All serious operas written this century are boring!

[*They turn and look at him in shocked amazement. A pause. He gives his little giggle, and then jumps down again.*]

Look at us! Four gaping mouths. What a perfect quartet! I'd love to write it – just this second of time, this *now*, as you are! Herr

Chamberlain thinking 'Impertinent Mozart: I must speak to the Emperor at once!' Herr Prefect thinking 'Ignorant Mozart: debasing opera with his vulgarity!' Herr Court Composer thinking 'German Mozart: what can he finally know about music?' And Herr Mozart himself, in the middle, thinking 'I'm just a good fellow. Why do they all disapprove of me?' [*Excitedly to* VAN SWIETEN] That's why opera is important, Baron. Because it's realer than any play! A dramatic poet would have to put all those thoughts down one after another to represent this second of time. The composer can put them all down at once – and still make us hear each one of them. Astonishing device: a Vocal Quartet! [*More and more excited*] ... I tell you I want to write a finale lasting half an hour! A quartet becoming a quintet becoming a sextet. On and on, wider and wider – all sounds multiplying and rising together – and the together making a sound entirely new! ... I bet you that's how God hears the world. Millions of sounds ascending at once and mixing in His ear to become an unending music, unimaginable to us! [*To* SALIERI] That's our job! That's our job, we composers: to combine the inner minds of him and him and him, and her and her – the thoughts of chambermaids and Court Composers – and turn the audience into God.

[*Pause.* SALIERI *stares at him fascinated. Embarrassed,* MOZART *blows a raspberry and giggles.*]

I'm sorry. I talk nonsense all day: it's incurable – ask Stanzerl. [*To* VAN SWIETEN] My tongue is stupid. My heart isn't.

VAN SWIETEN: No. You're a good fellow under all your nonsense: I know that. He'll make a fine new Brother, won't he, Salieri?

SALIERI: Better than I, Baron.

VAN SWIETEN: Just try, my friend, to be more serious with your gifts.

[*He smiles, presses* MOZART's *hand, and goes.* SALIERI *rises.*]

SALIERI: *Buona fortuna,* Mozart.

MOZART: *Grazie,* Signore. [*Rounding on* VON STRACK] Stop frowning, Herr Chamberlain. I'm a jackass. It's easy to be friends with a jackass: just shake his 'hoof'.

[*He forms his hand into a 'hoof'. Warily* VON STRACK *takes it –
then springs back as* MOZART *brays loudly like a donkey.*]

MOZART: *Hee-haw!* ... Tell the Emperor the opera's finished.

VON STRACK: Finished?

MOZART: Right here in my noddle. The rest's just scribbling.
Goodbye.

VON STRACK: Good-day to you.

MOZART: He's going to be proud of me. You'll see. [*He gives his
flourish of the hand and goes out, delighted with himself.*]

VON STRACK: That young man really is ...

SALIERI [*blandly*]: Very lively.

VON STRACK [*exploding*]: Intolerable ... *Intolerable!*

[VON STRACK *freezes in a posture of indignation.*]

SALIERI [*to audience*]: How could I stop it? ... How could I block
this opera of Figaro? ... Incredible to hear, within six weeks the
Creature had finished the entire score!

[ORSINI-ROSENBERG *bustles in.*]

ROSENBERG: Figaro is complete! The first performance will be on
May the first!

SALIERI: So soon?

ROSENBERG: There's no way we can stop it!

[*A slight pause.*]

SALIERI [*slyly*]: I have an idea. *Una piccola idea!*

ROSENBERG: What?

SALIERI: *Mi ha detto che c'è un balletto nel terzo atto?*

ROSENBERG [*puzzled*]: *Sí.*

VON STRACK: What does he say?

SALIERI: *E dimmi – non è vero che l'Imperatore ha proibito il balletto
nelle sue opere?*

ROSENBERG [*realizing*]: *Un balletto* ... Ah!

SALIERI: *Precisamente.*

ROSENBERG: *Oh, capisco! Ma che meraviglia! Perfetto!* [*He laughs in
delight.*] *Veramente ingegnoso!*

VON STRACK [*irritated*]: What is it? What is he suggesting?

SALIERI: See him at the theatre.

ROSENBERG: Of course. Immediately. I'd forgotten. You are brilliant, Court Composer.

SALIERI: I? ... I have said nothing. [*He moves away upstage.*]

[*The light begins to change, dimming down.*]

VON STRACK [*very cross*]: I must tell you that I resent this extremely. Mozart is right in some things. There is far too much Italian *chittero-chattero* at this Court! Now please to inform me at once, what was just said?

ROSENBERG [*lightly*]: *Pazienza*, my dear Chamberlain. *Pazienza*. Just wait and see!

[*From upstage* SALIERI *beckons to* VON STRACK. *Baffled and cross, the* CHAMBERLAIN *joins him. They watch together, unseen. The light dims further.*]

*   *   *

AN UNLIT THEATRE

[*In the background a projection of lamps glowing faintly in the darkened auditorium.* ORSINI-ROSENBERG *sits on one of the gold chairs, centre.*

MOZART *comes in quickly from the left, wearing another bright coat, and carrying the score of* Figaro. *He crosses to the fortepiano.*]

ROSENBERG: Mozart ... *Mozart!*

MOZART: Yes, Herr Director.

ROSENBERG [*agreeably*]: A word with you, please. Right away.

MOZART: Certainly. What is it?

ROSENBERG: I would like to see your score of *Figaro*.

MOZART: Oh yes. Why?

ROSENBERG: Just bring it here to me. [*Unmoving*] Into my hand, please.

[MOZART *hands it to him, puzzled.* ORSINI-ROSENBERG *turns the pages.*]

Now tell me: did you not know that His Majesty has expressly forbidden ballet in his operas?

MOZART: Ballet?

ROSENBERG: Such as occurs in your third act.

MOZART: That is not a ballet, Herr Director. That is a dance at Figaro's wedding.

ROSENBERG: Exactly. A dance.

MOZART [*trying to control himself*]: But, the Emperor doesn't mean to prohibit dancing when it's part of the story. He made that law to prevent insertions of stupid ballet like in French operas, and quite right too.

ROSENBERG [*raising his voice*]: It is not for you, Herr Mozart, to interpret the Emperor's edicts. Merely to obey them. [*He seizes the offending pages between his fingers.*]

MOZART: What are you doing? ... What are you doing, Excellency?

ROSENBERG: Taking out what should never have been put in.

[*In a terrible silence* ROSENBERG *tears out the pages.* MOZART *watches in disbelief. Upstage* SALIERI *and* VON STRACK *look on together from the dimness.*]

Now, sir, perhaps in future you will obey Imperial commands.

[*He tears out some more pages.*]

MOZART: But ... But – if all that goes – there'll be a hole right at the climax of the story! ... [*Crying out suddenly*] *Salieri! This is Salieri's idea!*

ROSENBERG: Don't be absurd.

SALIERI [*to audience*]: How did he think of that? Nothing I had ever done could possibly make him think of that on his own. Had God given him the idea?!

MOZART: It's a conspiracy. I can smell it. I can smell it!

ROSENBERG: Control yourself!

MOZART [*howling*]: *But what do you expect me to do?* The first performance is two days off!

ROSENBERG: Write it over. That's your forte, is it not? – writing at speed.

MOZART: Not when the music's *perfect*! Not when it's absolutely perfect as it is! ... [*Wildly*] I shall appeal to the Emperor! I'll go to him myself! I'll hold a rehearsal especially for him.

ROSENBERG: The Emperor does not attend rehearsals.

MOZART: He'll attend this one. Make no mistake – he'll come to this one! Then he'll deal with *you*!

ROSENBERG: This issue is simple. Write your act again today – or withdraw the opera. That's final.

[*Pause. He hands back the mutilated score to its composer.* MOZART *is shaking.*]

MOZART: You shit-pot.

[ORSINI-ROSENBERG *turns and walks imperturbably away from him.*]

Woppy, foppy, wet-arsed, Italian-loving shit-pot!

[*Serenely,* ORSINI-ROSENBERG *leaves the stage.*]

[*Screeching after him*] Count Orsini-Rosenshit! ... Rosencunt! ... Rosenbugger! ... I'll hold a rehearsal! You'll see! The Emperor will come! You'll see! You'll see! ... *You'll see!!* [*He throws down his score in a storm of hysterical rage.*]

[*Upstage in the dimness* VON STRACK *goes out, and* SALIERI *ventures down towards the shrieking little man.* MOZART *suddenly becomes aware of him. He turns, his hand shooting out in an involuntary gesture of accusation.*]

MOZART [*to* SALIERI]: I am *forbidden!* ... I am – forbidden! ... But of course you know already!

SALIERI [*quietly*]: Know what?

[MOZART *flings away from him.*]

MOZART [*bitterly*]: No matter!

SALIERI [*always blandly*]: Mozart, permit me. If you wish, I will speak to the Emperor myself. Ask him to attend a rehearsal.

MOZART [*amazed*]: You wouldn't.

SALIERI: I cannot promise he will come – but I can try.

MOZART: Sir! –

SALIERI: Good-day. [*He puts up his hands, barring further intimacy.*]

[MOZART *retreats to the fortepiano.*]

[*To audience*] Needless to say I did nothing whatever in the matter. Yet – to my total stupefaction –

[VON STRACK *and* ORSINI-ROSENBERG *hurry on downstage.*]
– in the middle of the last rehearsal of *Figaro* next day ...
[*The* EMPEROR JOSEPH *comes on from upstage.*]
JOSEPH [*cheerfully*]: Fêtes and fireworks! Fêtes and fireworks! Gentlemen, good afternoon!

* * *

THE THEATRE

SALIERI [*to audience*]: Entirely against his usual practice, the Emperor appeared!
[VON STRACK *and* ORSINI-ROSENBERG *look at each other in consternation.* JOSEPH *seats himself excitedly on one of the gold chairs, facing out front. As with the premiere of* Seraglio *seen in Act I, he watches the audience as if it were the opera.*]
JOSEPH: I can't wait for this, Mozart, I assure you! *Je prévois des merveilles!*
MOZART [*bowing fervently*]: Majesty!
[*The* COURTIERS *sit also:* VON STRACK *on his right-hand side,* ORSINI-ROSENBERG *on his left.* SALIERI *also sits, near the keyboard.*]
SALIERI [*to audience*]: What did this mean? Was this proof God had finally decided to defend Mozart against me? Was He engaging with me at last?
[MOZART *passes behind* SALIERI.]
MOZART [*earnestly, sotto voce*]: I am so grateful to you, I cannot express it!
SALIERI [*aside, to him*]: Hush. Say nothing.
[MOZART *goes on quickly to the fortepiano and sits at it.*]
[*to audience*]: One thing about the event certainly seemed more than coincidence.
[*Music sounds faintly: the end of the third act of* Figaro, *just before the dance music starts.*]
Strangely, His Majesty had arrived at precisely the moment when

the dancers would have begun, had not they and their music been
entirely cut.

[*The music stops abruptly.*]

He and all of us watched the action proceed in total silence.

[*Flanked by his* COURTIERS, *the* EMPEROR *stares out front, following
with his eyes what is obviously a silent pantomime. His face ex-
presses bewilderment.* ORSINI-ROSENBERG *watches his sovereign
anxiously. Finally the monarch speaks.*]

JOSEPH: I don't understand. Is it modern?

MOZART [*jumping up nervously from the keyboard*]: No, Majesty.

JOSEPH: Then what?

MOZART: The Herr Director has removed a dance that would have
occurred at this point.

JOSEPH [*to* ORSINI-ROSENBERG]: Why was this done?

ROSENBERG: It's your own regulation, Sire. No ballet in your opera.

MOZART: Majesty, this is not a ballet. It is part of a wedding feast:
entirely necessary for the story.

JOSEPH: Well, it certainly looks very odd the way it is. I can't say I
like it.

MOZART: Nor do I, Majesty.

JOSEPH: Do you like it, Rosenberg?

ROSENBERG: It's not a question of liking, Majesty. Your own law
decrees it.

JOSEPH: Yes. All the same, this is nonsense. Look at them: they're
like waxworks up there.

ROSENBERG: Well, not exactly, Majesty.

JOSEPH: I don't like waxworks.

MOZART: Nor do I, Majesty.

JOSEPH: Well, who would? What do you say, Salieri?

SALIERI: Italians are fond of waxworks, Majesty. [*Pause.*] Our
religion is largely based upon them.

JOSEPH: You are *cattivo* again, Court Composer.

VON STRACK [*intervening creamily*]: Your Majesty, Count Rosenberg
is very worried that if this music is put back it will create the
most unfortunate precedent. One will have thereafter to endure
hours of dancing in opera.

JOSEPH: I think we can guard against that, you know, Chamberlain.
I really think we can guard against hours of dancing. [*To* ORSINI-
ROSENBERG] Please restore Herr Mozart's music.

ROSENBERG: But Majesty, I must insist —

JOSEPH [*with a touch of anger*]: You will oblige me, Rosenberg! I wish
to hear Mozart's music. Do you understand me?

ROSENBERG: Yes, Majesty.

[MOZART *explodes with joy, jumps over a chair and throws himself
at* JOSEPH's *feet.*]

MOZART: Oh God, I thank your Majesty! [*He kisses the* EMPEROR's
hand extravagantly, as at their first meeting.] Oh thank you — thank
you — thank you Sire, forever!

JOSEPH [*withdrawing hand*]: Yes, yes — very good. A little less
enthusiasm, I beg you!

MOZART [*abashed*]: Excuse me.

[*The* EMPEROR *rises. All follow suit.*]

JOSEPH: Well. *There it is!*

* * *

THE FIRST PERFORMANCE OF *Figaro*

[*The theatre glows with light for the first performance of* Figaro.
COURTIERS *and* CITIZENS *come in swiftly.*
The EMPEROR *and his Court resume their seats and the others quickly
take theirs. In the front row we note* KATHERINA CAVALIERI, *all plumes
and sequins, and* KAPELLMEISTER BONNO—*older than ever. Behind them
sit* CONSTANZE *and the* VENTICELLI. *All of them stare out at the audience
as if it were the opera they have come to see: people of fashion down front;
poorer people crowded into the Light Box upstage.*
SALIERI *crosses as he speaks to where two chairs have been placed side by
side apart from the rest, on the left, to form his box. On the chair upstage
sits his good wife* TERESA — *more statuesque than ever.*]

SALIERI [*to audience*]: And so *Figaro* was produced in spite of all my efforts. I sat in my box and watched it happen. A conspicuous defeat for me. And yet I was strangely excited.

[*Faintly we hear Figaro singing the tune of 'Non più andrai'. The stage audience is obviously delighted: they smile out front as they watch the (invisible) action.*]

My March! My poor March of Welcome – now set to enchant the world forever!

[*It fades. Applause. The* EMPEROR *rises, and with him the audience, to denote an Intermission.* JOSEPH *greets* KATHERINA *and* BONNO. ORSINI-ROSENBERG *and* VON STRACK *go to* SALIERI'*s box.*]

ROSENBERG [*to* SALIERI]: Almost in your style, that last bit. But more vulgar of course. Far more obvious than you would ever be.

VON STRACK [*drawling*]: Exactly!

[*A bell rings for the end of the Intermission. The* EMPEROR *returns quickly to his seat. The audience sits. A pause. All look out front, unmoving.*]

SALIERI [*raptly and quietly: to audience*]: Trembling, I heard the second act. [*Pause.*] The restored third act. [*Pause.*] The astounding fourth. What shall I say to you who will one day hear this last act for yourselves? You will – because whatever else shall pass away, this must remain.

[*Faintly we hear the solemn closing ensemble from Act IV of* Figaro, '*Ah! Tutti contenti. Saremo cosi*'.]

[*Over this*] The scene was night in a summer garden. Pinprick stars gleamed down on shaking summerhouses. Plotters glided behind pasteboard hedges. I saw a woman, dressed in her maid's clothes, hear her husband utter the first tender words he has offered her in years only because he thinks she is someone else. Could one catch a realer moment? And how except in a net of pure artifice? The disguises of opera had been invented for Mozart. [*He can barely look out at the 'stage'.*] The final reconciliation melted sight. [*Pause.*] Through my tears I saw the Emperor yawn.

[JOSEPH *yawns. The music fades. There is scant applause.* JOSEPH *rises and the* COURTIERS *follow suit.* MOZART *bows.*]

JOSEPH [*coolly*]: Most ingenious, Mozart. You are coming along nicely ... I do think we must omit encores in future. It really makes things far too long. Make a note, Rosenberg.

ROSENBERG: Majesty.

[MOZART *lowers his head, crushed.*]

JOSEPH: Gentleman, good night to you. Strack, attend me.

[JOSEPH *goes out, with* VON STRACK. *Director* ORSINI-ROSENBERG *gives* MOZART *one triumphant look and follows.* SALIERI *nods to his wife who leaves with the audience. Only* CONSTANZE *lingers for a second, then she too goes. A pause.* MOZART *and* SALIERI *are left alone:* SALIERI *deeply shaken by the opera,* MOZART *deeply upset by its reception. He crosses and sits next to* SALIERI.]

MOZART [*low*]: Herr Salieri.

SALIERI: Yes?

MOZART: What do you think? Do you think I am coming along nicely?

SALIERI [*moved*]: I think the piece is ... extraordinary. I think it is ... *marvellous.* Yes.

[*Pause.* MOZART *turns to him.*]

MOZART: I'll tell you what it is. It's the best opera yet written. That's what it is. And only I could have done it. No one else living!

[SALIERI *turns his head swiftly, as if he has been slapped.* MOZART *rises and walks away. The light changes. The* VENTICELLI *rush on.* SALIERI *and* MOZART *both freeze.*]

VENTICELLO I: Rosenberg is furious.

VENTICELLO 2: He'll never forgive Mozart.

VENTICELLO I: He'll do anything to get back at him!

SALIERI [*rising: to audience*]: So it wasn't hard to get the piece cancelled. I saw to it through the person of the resentful Director that in the entire year *Figaro* was played only *nine times!* ... My defeat finally turned into a victory. And God's response to my challenge remained as inscrutable as ever ... Was He taking any notice of me *at all?* ...

[MOZART *breaks his freeze and comes downstage.*]

MOZART: *Withdrawn!* Absolutely no plans for its revival!

SALIERI: I commiserate with you, my friend. But if the public does not like one's work, one has to accept the fact gracefully. [*Aside, to audience*] And certainly they didn't.

VENTICELLO 1 [*complaining*]: It's too complicated!

VENTICELLO 2 [*complaining*]: Too tiresome!

VENTICELLO 1: All those morbid harmonies!

VENTICELLO 2: And never a good bang at the end of songs so you know when to clap!

[*The* VENTICELLI *go off.*]

SALIERI [*to audience*]: Obviously I would not need to plot too hard against his operas in future. I must concentrate on the man. I decided to see him as much as possible: to learn everything I could of his weaknesses.

✱　✱　✱

THE WALDSTÄDTEN LIBRARY

[SERVANTS *again bring on the wing-chair.*]

MOZART: I'll go to England. England loves music. That's the answer!

SALIERI [*to audience*]: We were yet again in the library of the Baroness Waldstädten: that room fated to be the scene of ghastly encounters between us. Again, too, the compensating *crema al mascarpone.*

[*He sits in the chair and eats greedily.*]

MOZART: I was there when I was a boy. They absolutely adored me. I had more kisses than you've had cakes! ... When I was a child, people loved me.

SALIERI: Perhaps they will again. Why don't you go to London and try?

MOZART: Because I have a wife and child and no money. I wrote to Papa to take the boy off my hands just for a few months so I could go – and he refused! ... He's a bitter man, of course. After he'd finished showing me off around Europe he never went anywhere himself. He just stayed up in Salzburg year after year, kissing the ring of the Fartsbishop and lecturing *me*! ... [*Confidentially*] The real thing is, you see, he's jealous. Under everything he's jealous of me! He'll never forgive me for being cleverer than he is.

[*He leans excitedly over* SALIERI's *chair like a naughty child.*]
I'll tell you a secret. Leopold Mozart is just a jealous, dried-up old turd ... And I actually detest him.

[*He giggles guiltily. The* VENTICELLI *appear quickly, and address* SALIERI, *as* MOZART *freezes.*]
VENTICELLO I [*solemnly*]: Leopold Mozart —
VENTICELLO 2 [*solemnly*]: Leopold Mozart —
VENTICELLO I and VENTICELLO 2: Leopold Mozart is dead!

[*They go off.* MOZART *recoils. A long pause.*]
SALIERI: Do not despair. Death is inevitable, my friend.
MOZART [*desperately*]: How will I go now?
SALIERI: What do you mean?
MOZART: In the world. There's no one else. No one who understands the wickedness around. *I can't see it!* ... He watched for me all my life — and I betrayed him.
SALIERI: No!
MOZART: I talked against him.
SALIERI: No!
MOZART [*distressed*]: I married where he begged me not. I left him alone. I danced and played billiards and fooled about, and he sat by himself night after night in an empty house, and no woman to care for him ...

[SALIERI *rises in concern.*]
SALIERI: Wolfgang. My dear Wolfgang. Don't accuse yourself! ... Lean upon me, if you care to ... Lean upon me.

[SALIERI *opens his arms in a wide gesture of paternal benevolence.* MOZART *approaches, and is almost tempted to surrender to the embrace. But at the last moment he avoids it, and breaks away down front, to fall on his knees.*]

77

MOZART: *Papa!*

SALIERI [*to audience*]: So rose the Ghost Father in *Don Giovanni!*

*   *   *

[*The two grim chords which open the Overture to* Don Giovanni *sound through the theatre.* MOZART *seems to quail under them, as he stares out front. On the backdrop in the Light Box appears the silhouette of a giant black figure, in cloak and tricorne hat. It extends its arms, menacingly and engulfingly, towards its begetter.*]

SALIERI: A Father more accusing than any in opera. So rose the figure of a Guilty Libertine, cast into Hell! ... I looked on astounded as from his ordinary life he made his art. We were both ordinary men, he and I. Yet he from the ordinary created legends – and I from legends created only the ordinary.

     [*The figure fades.* SALIERI *stands over the kneeling* MOZART.]
Could I not have stopped my war? Shown him some pity? Oh yes, my friends, at any time – if He above had shown me one drop of it! Every day I set to work I prayed – I still prayed, you understand – 'Make this one good in my ears! Just this one! *One!*' But would He ever? ... I heard my music calmed in convention – not one breath of spirit to lift it off the shallows. And I heard *his* –
     [*We hear the exquisite strains of the* terzetto '*Soave sia il vento' from* Così Fan Tutte.]
– the spirit singing through it unstoppable to my ears alone! [*To God, in anguish*] 'Grant this to me! ... *Grant this to me!* ... [*As 'God'*] 'No, no, no: I do not need you, Salieri! I have Mozart! Better for you to be silent!' *Hahahahaha!*
     [*The music cuts off as he giggles savagely.*]
The Creature's dreadful giggle was the laughter of God. I had to end it. But how? There was only one way. *Starvation.* Reduce the man to destitution. Starve out the God.

*   *   *

SALIERI [*to* MOZART]: How do you fare today?

MOZART: Badly. I have no money, and no prospect of any.

SALIERI: It would not be too hard, surely.

> [*Lights up on the Palace of Schönbrunn. The* EMPEROR *stands in the Light Box, in his golden space.*]

JOSEPH: We must find him a Post.

SALIERI [*to audience*]: One danger! The Emperor.

> [SALIERI *goes upstage to* JOSEPH.]

There's nothing available, Majesty.

JOSEPH: There's Chamber Composer now that Gluck is dead.

SALIERI [*shocked*]: Mozart to follow Gluck?

JOSEPH: I won't have him say I drove him away. You know what a tongue he has.

SALIERI: Then grant him Gluck's post, Majesty, but not his salary. That would be wrong.

JOSEPH: Gluck got two thousand florins a year. What should Mozart get?

SALIERI: Two hundred. Light payment, yes, but for light duties.

JOSEPH: Perfectly fair. I'm obliged to you, Court Composer.

SALIERI [*bowing*]: Majesty.

> [*Lights down a little on* JOSEPH *who still stands there.* SALIERI *returns to* MOZART.]

[*To audience*] Easily done. Like many men obsessed with being thought generous, the Emperor Joseph was quintessentially mean.

> [MOZART *kneels before the* EMPEROR.]

JOSEPH: Herr Mozart. *Vous nous faites honneur!* ...

> [*Lights out on the Court.* MOZART *turns and walks downstage.*]

MOZART: It's a damned insult! Not enough to keep a mouse in cheese for a week!

SALIERI: Regard it as a token, *caro* Herr.

MOZART: When I was young they gave me snuff-boxes. Now it's

tokens! And for what? Pom-pom, for fireworks! Twang-twang
for contredanzes!

SALIERI: I'm sorry it's made you angry. I'd not have suggested it if
I'd known you'd be distressed.

MOZART: You suggested it?

SALIERI: I regret I was not able to do more.

MOZART: Oh ... forgive me! You're a good man! I see that now!
You're a truly kind man − and I'm a monstrous fool!

[*He grasps* SALIERI's *hand.*]

SALIERI: No, please ...

MOZART: You make me ashamed ... You excellent man!

SALIERI: No, no, no, no, no, − *s'il vous plaît.* A little less enthusiasm
I beg you!

[MOZART *laughs delightedly at this imitation of the* EMPEROR.
SALIERI *joins in.* MOZART *suddenly doubles over with stomach
cramps. He groans.*]

Wolfgang! What is it?

MOZART: I get cramps sometimes in my stomach.

SALIERI: I'm sorry.

MOZART: Excuse me ... it's nothing really.

SALIERI: I will see you soon again?

MOZART: Of course.

SALIERI: Why not visit me?

MOZART: I will ... I promise!

SALIERI: *Bene.*

MOZART: *Bene.*

SALIERI: My friend. My new friend.

[MOZART *giggles with pleasure and goes off. A pause.*]

[*To audience*] Now if ever was the moment for God to crush me.
I waited − and do you know what happened? I had just ruined
Mozart's career at Court: God rewarded me by granting my dearest
wish!

[*The* VENTICELLI *come on.*]

VENTICELLO 1: Kapellmeister Bonno.

VENTICELLO 2: Kapellmeister Bonno.

VENTICELLO 1 and VENTICELLO 2: Kapellmeister Bonno is dead!
[SALIERI *opens his mouth in surprise.*]
VENTICELLO 1: You are appointed –
VENTICELLO 2: By Royal Decree –
VENTICELLO 1: To fill his place.
[*Lights full up on the* EMPEROR *at the back. He is flanked by* VON STRACK *and* ORSINI-ROSENBERG, *standing like icons as at their first appearance.*]
JOSEPH [*formally as* SALIERI *turns and bows to him*]: First Royal and Imperial Kapellmeister to our Court.
[*The* VENTICELLI *applaud.*]
VENTICELLO 1: Bravo.
VENTICELLO 2: Bravo.
ROSENBERG: *Evviva*, Salieri!
VON STRACK: Well done, Salieri!
JOSEPH [*warmly*]: Dear Salieri – There it is!
[*The lights go down on Schönbrunn. In the dark the* EMPEROR *and his Court leave the stage for the last time.* SALIERI *turns round, alarmed.*]
SALIERI [*to audience*]: I was now truly alarmed. How long would I go unpunished?
VENTICELLO 1: Mozart looks appalling.
VENTICELLO 2: It must be galling of course.
VENTICELLO 1: I hear he's dosing himself constantly with medicine.
SALIERI: For what?
VENTICELLO 2: Envy, I imagine.

★   ★   ★

THE PRATER

[*Fresh green trees appear on the backdrop. The light changes to yellow, turning the blue surround into a rich verdant green.*

MOZART *and* CONSTANZE *enter arm-in-arm. She is palpably pregnant and wears a poor coat and bonnet; his clothes are poorer too.* SALIERI *promenades with the* VENTICELLI.]

SALIERI: I met him next in the Prater.

MOZART [*to* SALIERI]: Congratulations, sir!

SALIERI: I thank you. And to you both! [*To audience*] Clearly there was a change for the worse. His eyes gleamed, oddly, like a dog's when the light catches. [*To* MOZART] I hear you are not well, my friend.

    [*He acknowledges* CONSTANZE, *who curtsies to him.*]

MOZART: I'm not. My pains stay with me.

SALIERI: How wretched. What can they be?

MOZART: Also, I sleep badly ... I have .., bad dreams.

CONSTANZE [*warningly*]: Wolferl!

SALIERI: Dreams?

MOZART: Always the same one ... A figure comes to me cloaked in grey – doing this. [*He beckons slowly*]. It has no face. Just grey – like a mask ... [*He giggles nervously.*] What can it mean, do you ˋ think?

SALIERI: Surely you do not believe in dreams?

MOZART: No of course not – really!

SALIERI: Surely *you* do not, Madame?

CONSTANZE: I never dream, sir. Things are unpleasant enough to me, awake.

    [SALIERI *bows.*]

MOZART: It's all fancy, of course!

CONSTANZE: If Wolfgang had proper work he might dream less, First Kapellmeister.

MOZART [*embarrassed, taking her arm*]: Stanzi, please! ... Excuse us, sir. Come, dearest. We are well enough, thank you!

    [*Husband and wife go off.*]

VENTICELLO I: He's growing freakish.

VENTICELLO 2: No question.

VENTICELLO 1: Grey figures with no faces!

SALIERI [*looking after him*]: He broods on his father too much, I fancy. Also his circumstances make him anxious.

VENTICELLO 1: They've moved house again.

VENTICELLO 2: To the Rauhensteingasse. Number nine hundred and seventy.

VENTICELLO 1: They must be desperate.

VENTICELLO 2: It's a real slum.

SALIERI: Does he earn any money at all, apart from his Post?

VENTICELLO 1: Nothing whatever.

VENTICELLO 2: I hear he's starting to beg.

VENTICELLO 1: They say he's written letters to twenty Brother Masons.

SALIERI: Really?

VENTICELLO 2: And they're giving him money.

SALIERI [*to audience*]: Of course! They *would*! ... I had *forgotten* the Masons! *Naturally* they would relieve him – *how stupid of me*! ... There could be no finally starving him with the Masons there to help! As long as he asked they would keep supplying his wants ... How could I stop it? And quickly! ...

VENTICELLO 1: Lord Fugue is most displeased with him!

SALIERI: *Is* he?

* * *

A MASONIC LODGE

[*A huge golden emblem descends, encrusted with Masonic symbols. Enter* VAN SWIETEN. *He is wearing the ritual apron over his sober clothes. At the same time* MOZART *enters from the left. He too wears the apron. The two men clasp hands in fraternal greeting.*]

VAN SWIETEN [*gravely*]: This is not good, Brother. The Lodge was not created for you to beg from.

MOZART: What else can I do?

VAN SWIETEN: Give concerts, as you used to do.

MOZART: I have no subscribers left, Baron. I am no longer fashionable.

VAN SWIETEN: I am not surprised. You write tasteless comedies which give offence. I warned you, often enough.

MOZART [*humbly*]: You did. I admit it. [*He holds his stomach in pain.*]

VAN SWIETEN: I will send you some fugues of Bach tomorrow. You can arrange those for my Sunday Concert. You shall have a small fee.

MOZART: Thank you, Baron.

> [VAN SWIETEN *nods and goes out.* SALIERI *steps forward. He again wears the Masonic apron.*]

[*shouting after* VAN SWIETEN] I cannot live by arranging Bach!

SALIERI [*sarcastically*]: A generous fellow.

MOZART: All the same, I'll have to do it. If he were to turn the Lodge against me, I'd be finished. My Brother Masons virtually keep me now ... Never mind. I'll manage: you'll see! Things are looking up already. I've had a marvellous proposal from Schikaneder. He's a new Member of this Lodge.

SALIERI: Schikaneder? The actor?

MOZART: Yes. He owns a theatre in the suburbs.

SALIERI: Well, more of a music-hall, surely?

MOZART: Yes ... He wants me to write him a Vaudeville – something for ordinary German people. Isn't that a wonderful idea? ... He's offered me half the receipts when we open.

SALIERI: Nothing in advance?

MOZART: He said he couldn't afford anything. I know it's not much of an offer. But a popular piece about Brotherly Love could celebrate everything we believe as Masons!

SALIERI: It certainly could! ... Why don't you put the Masons *into* it?

MOZART: Into an opera? ... I couldn't!

   [SALIERI *laughs, to indicate that he was simply making a joke.*]
   All the same – what an idea!

SALIERI [*earnestly*]: Our rituals are secret, Wolfgang.

MOZART: I needn't copy them exactly. I could adapt them a little.

SALIERI: Well ... It would certainly be in a great cause.

MOZART: Brotherly Love!

SALIERI: Brotherly Love!

   [*They both turn and look solemnly at the great golden emblem hanging
   at their back.*]

   [*Warmly*] Take courage, Wolfgang. It's a glorious idea.

MOZART: It is, isn't it? It *really is*!

SALIERI: Of course say nothing till it's done.

MOZART: Not a word.

SALIERI [*making a sign: closed fist*]: Secret!

MOZART [*making a similar sign*]: Secret!

SALIERI: Good.

   [*He steps out of the scene downstage.*]

   [*To audience*] And if that didn't finish him off with the Masons –
nothing would!

   [*The gold emblem withdraws. We hear the merry dance of Monostatos
and the hypnotized slaves from* The Magic Flute: *'Das Klinget so
herrlich, Das Klinget so schön!' To the tinkling of the glockenspiel*
SERVANTS *bring in a long plain table loaded with manuscripts and
bottles. It also bears a plain upturned stool. They place this in the
wooden area head-on to the audience. At the same time* CONSTANZE
*appears wearily from the back, and enters this apartment: the
Rauhensteingasse. She wears a stuffed apron, indicating the advanced
state of her pregnancy. Simultaneously upstage left, two other*
SERVANTS *have placed the little gilded table bearing a loaded cake-
stand and three of the gilded chairs from* SALIERI's *resplendent Salon.
We now have in view the two contrasting apartments.
As soon as the emblem withdraws, the* VENTICELLI *appear to*
SALIERI.]

*   *   *

MOZART'S APARTMENT: SALIERI'S APARTMENT

VENTICELLO 1: Mozart is delighted with himself!

VENTICELLO 2: He's writing a secret opera!

VENTICELLO 1 [*crossly*]: And won't tell anyone its theme.

VENTICELLO 2: It's really too tiresome.

    [*The* VENTICELLI *go off.*]

SALIERI: He told *me*. He told me everything! ... Initiation ceremonies. Ceremonies with blindfolds. All rituals copied from the Masons ... He sat at home preparing his own destruction. A home where life grew daily more grim.

    [*He goes upstage and sits on one of his gilded chairs, devouring a cake.* MOZART *also sits at his table, wrapped in a blanket, and starts to write music. Opposite him* CONSTANZE *sits on a stool, wrapped in a shawl.*]

CONSTANZE: I'm cold ... I'm cold all day ... Hardly surprising since we have no firewood.

MOZART: Papa was right. We end exactly as he said. Beggars.

CONSTANZE: It's all his fault.

MOZART: What do you mean?

CONSTANZE: He kept you a baby all your life.

MOZART: I don't understand ... You always loved Papa.

CONSTANZE: *I* did?

MOZART: You adored him. You told me so often.

    [*Slight pause.*]

CONSTANZE [*flatly*]: I hated him.

MOZART: What?

CONSTANZE: And he hated me.

MOZART: That's absurd. He loved us both very much. You're being extremely silly now.

CONSTANZE: Am I?

MOZART [*airily*]: Yes, you are, little-wife-of-my-heart!

CONSTANZE: Do you remember the fire we had last night, because it was so cold you couldn't even get the ink wet? You said 'What a blaze' – remember? 'What a blaze! All those old papers going up!' Well, my dear, those old papers were just all your father's letters, that's all – every one he wrote since the day we married.

MOZART: *What?*

CONSTANZE: Every one! All the letters about what a ninny I am – what a bad housekeeper I am! Every one!

MOZART [*crying out*]: Stanzi!

CONSTANZE: *Shit on him! ... Shit on him!*

MOZART: *You bitch!*

CONSTANZE [*savagely*]: At least it kept us warm! What else will do that? Perhaps we should dance! You love to dance, Wolferl – let's dance! Dance to keep warm! [*Grandly*] Write me a contredanze, Mozart! It's your job to write dances, isn't it?

    [*Hysterical, she starts dancing roughly round the room like a demented peasant to the tune of 'Non più andrai'.*]

    [*singing wildly*] Non più andrai, farfallone amoroso –
        Notte e giorno d'intorno girando!

MOZART [*shrieking*]: Stop it! Stop it! [*He seizes her.*] Stanzi-marini! Marini-bini! Don't please! Please, please, please I beg you ... Look there's a kiss! Where's it coming from? Right out of that corner! There's another one – all wet, all sloppy wet coming straight to *you*! Kiss – kiss – kiss!

    [*She pushes him away.* CONSTANZE *dances.* MOZART *catches her. She pushes him away.*]

CONSTANZE: Get off!

    [*Pause.*]

MOZART: I'm frightened, Stanzi. Something awful's happening to me.

CONSTANZE: I can't bear it. I can't bear much more of this.

MOZART: And the Figure's like this now – [*Beckoning faster*] 'Here! Come here! Here!' Its face still masked – invisible! It becomes realer and realer to me!

CONSTANZE: Stop it, for God's sake! ... Stop! ... It's me who's frightened ... *Me!* ... You frighten me ... If you go on like this I'll leave you. I swear it.

MOZART [*shocked*]: Stanzi!

CONSTANZE: I mean it ... I do ... [*She puts her hand to her stomach, as if in pain.*]

MOZART: I'm sorry ... Oh God, I'm sorry ... I'm sorry, I'm sorry, I'm sorry! ... Come here to me, little wife of my heart! Come ... Come ...

[*He kneels and coaxes her to him. She comes half-reluctantly, half-willingly.*]

MOZART: Who am I? ... Quick: tell me. Hold me and tell who I am.

CONSTANZE: Pussy-wussy.

MOZART: Who else?

CONSTANZE: Miaowy-powy.

MOZART: And you're squeeky-peeky. And Stanzi-manzi. And Binigini!

[*She surrenders.*]

CONSTANZE: Wolfi-polfi!

MOZART: Poopy-peepee!

[*They giggle.*]

CONSTANZE: Now don't be stupid.

MOZART [*insistent: like a child*]: Come on – do it. Do it – Let's do it. Poppy!

[*They play a private game, gradually doing it faster, on their knees.*]

CONSTANZE: Poppy.

MOZART [*changing it*]: Pappy.

CONSTANZE [*copying*]: Pappy.

MOZART: Pappa.

CONSTANZE: Pappa.

MOZART: Pappa-pappa!

CONSTANZE: Pappa-pappa!

MOZART: Pappa-pappa-pappa-pappa!

CONSTANZE: Pappa-pappa-pappa-pappa!

[*They rub noses.*]

TOGETHER: Pappa-pappa-pappa-pappa! Pappa-pappa-pappa-pappa!

CONSTANZE: *Ah!*

[*She suddenly cries out in distress, and clutches her stomach.*]

MOZART: Stanzi! ... Stanzi, what is it?

[*The* VENTICELLI *hurry in.*]

VENTICELLO I: News!

VENTICELLO 2: Suddenly!

VENTICELLO I: She's been delivered.

VENTICELLO 2: Unexpectedly.

VENTICELLO I: Of a boy.

VENTICELLO 2: Poor little imp.

VENTICELLO I: To be born to that couple.

VENTICELLO 2: In that room.

VENTICELLO I: With that money.

VENTICELLO 2: And the father a baby himself.

[*During the above,* CONSTANZE *has slowly risen and divested herself of her stuffed apron — thereby ceasing to be pregnant. Now she turns sorrowfully and walks slowly upstage and off it.* MOZART *follows her for a few steps, alarmed. He halts.*]

VENTICELLO I: And now I hear —

VENTICELLO 2: Now I hear —

VENTICELLO I: Something more has happened.

VENTICELLO 2: Even stranger.

[MOZART *picks up a bottle — then moves swiftly into* SALIERI's *room.*]

MOZART: *She's gone!*

SALIERI: What do you mean?

[*The* VENTICELLI *go off.* MOZART *moves up to* SALIERI's *apartment, holding his bottle, and sits on one of the gilded chairs.*]

MOZART: Stanzerl's gone away. Just for a while, she says. She's taken the baby and gone to Baden. To the spa. It will cost us the last money we have!

SALIERI: But *why?*

MOZART: She's right to go ... It's my fault ... She thinks I'm mad.

SALIERI: Surely not?

MOZART: Perhaps I am ... I think I am ... Yes ...

SALIERI: Wolfgang ...

MOZART: Let me tell you! Last night I saw the Figure again – the figure in my dreams. [*Very disturbed*] It stood before my table, all in grey, its face still grey, still masked. And this time it spoke to me! 'Wolfgang Mozart – you must write now a Requiem Mass. Take up your pen and begin!'

SALIERI: A Requiem? Who is this Requiem for?

MOZART: I asked 'Who has died?' It said, 'The work must be finished when you see me next!' Then it turned and left the room.

SALIERI: Oh, this is morbid fancy, my friend!

MOZART: It had the force of real things! ... To tell the truth – I do not know whether it happened in my head or out of it ... No wonder Stanzi has gone. I frightened her away ... And now she'll miss the vaudeville.

SALIERI: You mean it's finished? So soon?

MOZART: Oh yes – music is easy: it's marriage that's hard!

SALIERI: I long to see it!

MOZART: Would you come, truly? The theatre isn't grand. No one from Court will be there.

SALIERI: Do you think that matters to me? I would travel anywhere for a work by you! ... I am no substitute for your little wife – but I know someone who could be!

[*He gets up.* MOZART *rises also.*]

MOZART: Who?

SALIERI: I'll tell you what – I'll bring Katherina! She'll cheer you up!

MOZART: Katherina!

SALIERI: As I remember it, you quite enjoyed her company!

[MOZART *laughs heartily.* CAVALIERI *enters, now fatter and wearing an elaborate plumed hat. She curtsies to* MOZART *and takes his arm.*]

MOZART [*bowing*]: Signora!

SALIERI [*to audience*]: And so to the opera we went – a strange band of three!

[*The other two freeze.*]

The First Kapellmeister – sleek as a cat. His mistress – now fat and feathered like the great song-bird she'd become. And demented Mozart – drunk on the cheap wine which was now his constant habit.

[*They unfreeze and walk across the stage.*]

We went out into the suburbs – to a crowded music-hall – in a tenement!

* * *

THE THEATRE BY THE WEIDEN

[*Two benches are brought in and placed down front. Sudden noise. A crowd of working-class Germans swarm in from the back: a chattering mass of humanity through which the three have to push their way to the front. The long table is pushed horizontally, and the rowdy audience piles on top of it, smoking pipes and chewing sausages.*

Unobserved, BARON VAN SWIETEN *comes in also and stands at the back.*]

MOZART: You must be indulgent now! It's my first piece of this kind!

[*The three sit on the front bench:* MOZART *sick and emaciated;* CAVALIERI *blowsy and bedizened;* SALIERI *as elegant as ever.*]

SALIERI: We sat as he wished us to, among ordinary Germans! The smell of sweat and sausage was almost annihilating!

[CAVALIERI *presses a mouchoir to her sensitive nose.*]

[*To* MOZART] This is so exciting!

MOZART [*happily*]: Do you think so?

SALIERI [*looking about him*]: Oh yes! This is exactly the audience we should be writing for! Not the dreary Court ... As always – *you* show the way!

[*The audience freezes.*]

[*To us*] As always, he did. My pungent neighbours *rolled* on their benches at the jokes –

[*They unfreeze – briefly to demonstrate this mirth –*]

And I alone in their midst heard – *The Magic Flute!*

[*They freeze again. The great hymn at the end of Act II is heard:
'Heil sei euch Geweihten'.*]

He had put the Masons into it right enough. Oh yes – but how?
He had turned them into an Order of Eternal Priests. I heard voices
calling out of ancient temples. I saw a vast sun rise on a timeless
land, where animals danced and children floated: and by its rays all
the poisons we feed each other drawn up and burnt away!

[*A great sun does indeed rise inside the Light Box, and standing in
it the gigantic silhouette of a priestly figure extending its arms to the
world in universal greeting.*]

And in this sun – behold – I saw his father. No more an accusing
figure, but forgiving! The Highest Priest of the Order – his hand
extended to the world in love! Wolfgang feared Leopold no longer:
a final Legend has been made! . . . Oh the sound – the sound of that
new-found peace in him – mocking my undiminishing pain! *There*
was the Magic Flute – *there beside me!*

[*He points to* MOZART. *Applause from all.* MOZART *jumps up
excitedly on to the bench and acknowledges the clapping with his arms
flung out. He turns to us, a bottle in his hand – his eyes staring: all
freeze again.*]

SALIERI: Mozart the flute, and God the relentless player. How long
could the Creature stand it – so frail, so palpably mortal? And what
was this I was tasting suddenly? Could it be pity? . . . *Never!*

VAN SWIETEN [*calling out*]: Mozart!

[VAN SWIETEN *pushes his way to the front through the crowd of
dispersing* CITIZENS. *He is outraged.*]

MOZART [*turning joyfully to greet him*]: Baron! You here! How
wonderful of you to come!

SALIERI [*to audience*]: I had of course suggested it.

VAN SWIETEN [*with cold fury*]: What have you done?

MOZART: Excellency?

VAN SWIETEN: You have put our rituals into a vulgar show!

MOZART: No, sir –

VAN SWIETEN: They are plain for all to see! And to laugh at! You
have betrayed the Order.

MOZART [*in horror*]: *No!*

SALIERI: Baron, a word with you —

VAN SWIETEN: Don't speak for him, Salieri! [*To* MOZART, *with frozen contempt*] You were ever a cruel vulgarian we hoped to mend. Stupid, hopeless task! Now you are a betrayer as well. I shall never forgive you. And depend upon it — I shall ensure that no Freemason or Person of Distinction will do so in Vienna so long as I have life!

SALIERI: Baron, please, I must speak!

VAN SWIETEN: No, sir! Leave alone. [*To* MOZART] I did not look for this reward, Mozart. Never speak to me.

[*He goes out. The crowd disperses. The lights change. The benches are taken off.* SALIERI, *watching* MOZART *narrowly, dismisses* KATHERINA. MOZART *stands as one dead.*]

SALIERI: Wolfgang? ...

[MOZART *shakes his head sharply — and walks away from him, upstage, desolate and stunned.*]

Wolfgang — all is not lost.

[MOZART *enters his apartment and freezes.*]

[*To audience*] But of course it was! Now he was ruined. Broken and shunned by all men of influence. He did not even get his half receipts from the opera.

★   ★   ★

[*The* VENTICELLI *come in.*]

VENTICELLO 1: Schikaneder pays him nothing.

VENTICELLO 2: Schikaneder cheats him.

VENTICELLO 1: Gives him enough for liquor.

VENTICELLO 2: And keeps all the rest.

SALIERI: I couldn't have managed it better myself.

[MOZART *takes up a blanket and muffles himself in it. Then he sits at his work-table, down front, staring out at the audience, quite still, the blanket almost over his face.*]

And then silence. No word came from him at all. Why? ... I waited each day. Nothing. Why? . . . [*To the* VENTICELLI, *brusquely*] *What does he do?*

[MOZART *writes.*]

VENTICELLO 1: He sits at his window.

VENTICELLO 2: All day and all night.

VENTICELLO 1: Writing —

VENTICELLO 2: Writing — like a man possessed.

[MOZART *springs to his feet, and freezes.*]

VENTICELLO 1: Springs up every moment!

VENTICELLO 2: Stares wildly at the street!

VENTICELLO 1: Expecting something —

VENTICELLO 2: Someone —

VENTICELLO 1 and VENTICELLO 2: We can't imagine what!

SALIERI [*to audience*]: I could!

[*He also springs up excitedly, dismissing the* VENTICELLI. MOZART *and* SALIERI *now both stand staring out front.*]

Who did he look for? A Figure in grey, masked and sorrowing, come to take him away. I knew what he was doing, alone in that slum! He was writing his Requiem Mass — for himself! . . . And now I confess the wickedest thing I did to him.

[*His* VALET *brings him the clothes which he describes, and he puts them on, turning his back to us to don the hat — to which is attached a mask.*]

My friends — there is no blasphemy a man will not commit, compelled to such a war as mine! I got me a cloak of grey. Yes. And a mask of grey — Yes!

[*He turns round: he is masked.*]

and appeared myself to the demented Creature as — the *Messenger of God*! . . . I confess that in November seventeen ninety-one, I — Antonio Salieri, then as now First Kapellmeister to the Empire — walked empty Vienna in the freezing moonlight for seven nights on end! That precisely as the clocks of the city struck one I would halt beneath Mozart's window — and become his more terrible clock.

[*The clock strikes one.* SALIERI, *without moving from the left side of the stage, raises his arms: his fingers show seven days.* MOZART *rises – fascinated and appalled – and stands equally rigidly on the right side, looking out in horror.*]

Every night I showed him one day less – then stalked away. Every night the face he showed me at the glass was more crazed. Finally – with no days left to him – *horror!* I arrived as usual. Halted. And instead of fingers, reached up beseechingly as the Figure of his dreams! 'Come! – Come! – Come! ...'

[*He beckons to* MOZART, *insidiously.*]

He stood swaying, as if he would faint off into death. But suddenly – incredibly – he realized all his little strength, and in a clear voice called down to me the words of his opera *Don Giovanni*, inviting the statue to dinner.

MOZART [*pushing open the 'window'*]: *O statua gentilissima – venite a cena!*

[*He beckons in his turn.*]

SALIERI: For a long moment one terrified man looked at another. Then – unbelievably – I found myself nodding, just as in the opera. Starting to move across the street!

[*The rising and falling scale passage from the Overture to* Don Giovanni *sounds darkly, looped in sinister repetition. To this hollow music* SALIERI *marches slowly upstage.*]

Pushing down the latch of his door – tramping up the stairs with stone feet. There was no stopping it. *I was in his dream!*

[MOZART *stands terrified by his table.* SALIERI *throws open the door. An instant light change.*

SALIERI *stands still, staring impassively downstage.* MOZART *addresses him urgently, and in awe.*]

MOZART: It's not finished! ... Not nearly! ... Forgive me. Time was I could write a Mass in a week! ... Give me one month more, and it'll be done: I swear it! ... He'll grant me that, surely? God can't want it unfinished! ... Look – look, see what I've done.

[*He snatches up the pages from the table and brings them eagerly to the Figure.*]

Here's the Kyrie – that's finished! Take that to Him – He'll see it's not unworthy! ...

[*Unwillingly* SALIERI *moves across the room – takes the pages, and sits behind the table in* MOZART's *chair, staring out front.*]

Grant me time, I beg you! If you do, I swear I'll write a real piece of music. I know I've boasted I've written hundreds, but it's not true. I've written nothing finally good!

[SALIERI *looks at the pages. Immediately we hear the sombre opening of the Requiem Mass. Over this* MOZART *speaks.*]

Oh it began so well, my life. Once the world was so full, so happy! ... All the journeys – all the carriages – all the rooms of smiles! Everyone smiled at me once – the King at Schönbrunn; the Princess at Versailles. They lit my way with candles to the clavier! – my father bowing, bowing, bowing with such joy! 'Chevalier Mozart, my miraculous son!' ... Why has it all gone? ... Why? ... Was I so bad? So wicked? ... Answer for Him and tell me!

[*Deliberately* SALIERI *tears the paper into pieces. The music stops instantly. Silence.*]

[*Fearfully*] Why? ... Is it not good?

SALIERI [*stiffly*]: It is good. Yes. It is good.

[*He tears off a corner of the music paper, elevates it in the manner of the Communion Service, places it on his tongue and eats it.*]

[*In pain*] I eat what God gives me. Dose after dose. For all of life. His poison. We are both poisoned, Amadeus. I with you: you with me.

[*In horror* MOZART *moves slowly behind him, placing his hand over* SALIERI's *mouth – then, still from behind, slowly removes the mask and hat.* SALIERI *stares at us.*]

Eccomi. Antonio Salieri. Ten years of my hate have poisoned you to death.

[MOZART *falls to his knees, by the table.*]

MOZART: Oh God!

SALIERI [*contemptuously*]: *God?!* ... God will not help you! God *does* not help!

MOZART: Oh God! ... Oh God! ... On God!

SALIERI: God does not love you, Amadeus! God does not love! He can only *use*! ... He cares nothing for who He uses: nothing for who He denies! ... You are no use to Him any more – You're too weak – too sick! He has finished with you! All you can do now is *die*!

MOZART: *Ah!*

[*With a groan* MOZART *crawls quickly through the trestle of the table like an animal finding a burrow – or a child a safe place of concealment.* SALIERI *kneels by the table, calling in at his victim in desperation.*]

SALIERI: Die, Amadeus! Die, I beg you, die! ... Leave me alone, *ti imploro*! Leave me alone at last! Leave me alone!

[*He beats on the table in his despair.*]

Alone! Alone! Alone! Alone! Alone!

MOZART [*crying out at the top of his lungs*]: PAPAAAAA!

[*He freezes – his mouth open in the act of screaming – his head staring out from under the table.*

SALIERI *rises in horror. Silence. Then very slowly* MOZART *crawls out from under the table. He stares upwards. He sits. He smiles.*]

[*In a childish voice*] Papa!

[*Silence.*]

Papa ... papa ...

[*He extends his arms upwards, imploringly. He speaks now as a very young boy.*]

Take me, Papa. Take me. Put down your arms and I'll hop into them. Just as we used to do it! ... Hop-hop-hop-hop-UP!

[*He jumps up on to the table.* SALIERI *watches in horror.*]

Hold me close to you, Papa. Let's sing our little Kissing Song together. Do you remember? ...

[*He sings in an infantine voice.*]

Oragna figata fa! Marina gamina fa!

SALIERI: Reduce the man: reduce the God. Behold my vow fulfilled. The profoundest voice in the world reduced to a nursery tune.

[*He leaves the room, slowly, as* MOZART *resumes his singing.*]

MOZART: *Oragna figata fa! Marina gamina fa!*

[*As* SALIERI *withdraws,* CONSTANZE *appears from the back of the stage, her bonnet in her hand. She has returned from Baden. She comes downstage towards her husband, and finds him there on the table singing in an obviously childish treble.*]

Oragna figata fa! Marina gamina fa. Fa! Fa!

[*He kisses the air, several times. Finally he becomes aware of his wife standing beside him.*]

[*Uncertainly*] Stanzi?

CONSTANZE: Wolfi? ...

MOZART [*in relief*]: Stanzi!

CONSTANZE [*with great tenderness*]: Wolfi – my love! Little husband of my heart!

[*He virtually falls off the table into her arms.*]

MOZART: Oh!

[*He clings to her in overwhelming pleasure. She helps him gently to move around the table to the chair behind it, facing out front.*]

CONSTANZE: Oh, my dear one – come with me ... Come on ... Come on now. There ... There ...

[MOZART *sits weakly.*]

MOZART [*like a child still, and most earnestly*]: Salieri ... Salieri has killed me.

CONSTANZE: Yes, my dear.

[*Practically she busies herself clearing the table of its candle, its bottle and its inkwell.*]

MOZART: He has. He told me so.

CONSTANZE: Yes, yes: I'm sure.

[*She finds two pillows and places them at the left-hand head of the table.*]

MOZART [*petulantly*]: He did ... He did!

CONSTANZE: Hush now, lovey.

[*She helps her dying husband on to the table, now his bed. He lies down, and she covers him with her shawl.*]

I'm back to take care of you. I'm sorry I went away. I'm here now, for always!

MOZART: Salieri ... Salieri ... Salieri ... Salieri!

[*He starts to weep.*]

CONSTANZE: Oh lovey, be silent now. No one has hurt you. You'll get better soon, I promise. Can you hear me?

[*Faintly the Lacrimosa of the Requiem Mass begins to sound.* MOZART *rises to hear it — leaning against his wife's shoulders. His hand begins feebly to beat out drum measures from the music. During the whole of the following it is evident that he is composing the Mass in his head, and does not hear his wife at all.*]

You've got to get well, Wolfi — because we need you. Karl and Baby Franz as well. There's only the three of us, lovey: we don't cost much. Just don't leave us — we wouldn't know what to do without you. And you wouldn't know much either, up in Heaven, without us. You soppy thing. You can't even cut up your own meat without help! ... I'm not clever, lovey. It can't have been easy living with a goose. But I've looked after you, you must admit that. And I've given you fun too — quite a lot really! ... Are you listening?

[*The drum strokes get slower, and stop.*]

Know one thing. It was the best day of my life when you married me. And as long as I live I'll be the most honoured woman in the world ... Can you hear me?

[*She becomes aware that* MOZART *is dead. She opens her mouth in a silent scream, raising her arm in a rigid gesture of grief. The great chord of the 'Amen' does not resolve itself, but lingers on in intense reverberation.*]

*   *   *

[CITIZENS OF VIENNA *come in, dressed in black, from the right.* CONSTANZE *kneels and freezes in grief, as* SERVANTS *come in and stand at each of the four corners of the table on which the dead body lies.* VAN SWIETEN *also comes in.*]

SALIERI [*hard*]: The Death Certificate said kidney failure, hastened by exposure to cold. Generous Lord Fugue paid for a pauper's funeral. Twenty other corpses. An unmarked limepit.

[VAN SWIETEN *approaches* CONSTANZE.]

VAN SWIETEN: What little I can spare, you shall have for the children. There's no need to waste it on vain show.

[*The* SERVANTS *lift the table and bear it, with its burden, upstage, centre, to the Light Box. The* CITIZENS *follow it.*]

SALIERI: What did I feel? Relief, of course: I confess it. And pity too, for the man I helped to destroy. I felt the pity God can never feel. I weakened God's flute to thinness. God blew – as He must – without cease. The flute split in the mouth of His insatiable need.

[*The* CITIZENS *kneel. In dead silence the* SERVANTS *throw* MOZART's *body off the table into the space at the back of the stage. All depart save* SALIERI *and* CONSTANZE. *She unfreezes and starts assiduously collecting the manuscripts scattered over the floor.*

SALIERI *now speaks with an increasingly ageing voice: a voice poisoned more and more by his own bitterness.*]

As for Constanze, in the fullness of time she married again – a Danish diplomat as dull as a clock – and retired to Salzburg, birthplace of the Composer, to become the pious Keeper of his Shrine!

[CONSTANZE *rises, wrapping her shawl about her, and clasping manuscripts to her bosom.*]

CONSTANZE [*reverentially*]: A sweeter-tongued man never lived! In ten years of blissful marriage I never heard him utter a single coarse or conceited word. The purity of his life is reflected absolutely in the purity of his music! ... [*More briskly*] In selling his manuscripts I charge by the ink. So many notes, so many schillings. That seems to me the simplest way.

[*She leaves the stage, a pillar of rectitude.*]

SALIERI: One amazing fact emerged. Mozart did not *imagine* that masked Figure who said 'Take up your pen and write a Requiem.' It was *real*! ... A certain bizarre nobleman called Count Walsegg had a longing to be thought a composer. He actually sent his Steward in disguise to Mozart to commission the piece — secretly, so that he could pass it off as his own work. And this he even did! After Mozart's death it was actually performed as Count Walsegg's Requiem ... And I conducted it.

[*He smiles at the audience.*]

Naturally I did. In those days I presided over all great musical occasions in Vienna.

[*He divests himself of his cloak.*]

SALIERI: I even conducted the salvos of cannon in Beethoven's dreadful Battle Symphony. The experience made me almost as deaf as *he* was!

*   *   *.

[*The* CITIZENS *bow and kiss their hands to him.*]

SALIERI: So I remained in Vienna — City of Musicians — reverenced by all. And slowly I understood the nature of God's punishment! ... What had I begged for in that church as a boy? Was it not fame? ... Fame for excellence? ... Well now I had fame! I was to become — quite simply — the most famous musician in Europe!

[*All the* CITIZENS *fall on their knees before him, clapping their hands silently, and relentlessly extending their arms upwards and upwards, almost obliterating him.*]

I was to be bricked up in fame! Embalmed in fame! Buried in fame — but for work I knew to be *absolutely worthless*! ... This was my sentence: — I must endure thirty years of being called 'distinguished' by people incapable of distinguishing! ... and finally — his Masterstroke! When my nose had been rubbed in fame to vomiting — it would all be taken away from me. Every scrap.

[*The* CITIZENS *rise, and all walk away indifferently upstage, past him, on into the Light Box, and off the stage.*]

I must survive to see myself become extinct!

[*A* SERVANT *hands him his old stained dressing-gown and cap.*]
When they trundled me out to a carriage to get my last Award,
a man on the kerb said 'Isn't that one of the Generals from
Waterloo?'
[*The last movement of the Jupiter Symphony begins to sound, growing
ever louder.*]
Mozart's music sounded louder and louder through the world!
And mine faded completely, till no one played it at all! [*Yelling
upwards*] Nemico dei Nemici! Dio Implacabile!
[*The Mozart symphony wells to a huge crescendo, seeming to drown
SALIERI. He sinks to his knees under the weight of it, and finally
claps his hands to his aching ears to shut it out. The deafening music
snaps off. The curtains descend in a rush. A clock strikes six.*]

*   *   *

SALIERI'S APARTMENT
NOVEMBER 1823

[*A* SERVANT *comes in quickly with the wheelchair.* SALIERI *speaks again
in the voice of an old man.*]

SALIERI [*to audience*]: Dawn has come. I must release you – and myself.
One moment's violence and it's done. You see, I cannot accept
this. I did not live on earth to be His joke for Eternity. I *will*
be remembered! *I will be remembered!* – if not in fame, then infamy.
One moment more and I win battle with Him. Watch and see!
. . . All this month I've been shouting about murder. 'Have mercy,
Mozart! Pardon your Assassin!' And now my last move. A false
confession – short and convincing!
[*He pulls it out of his pocket.*]
How I really did murder Mozart – with arsenic – out of envy!
And how I cannot live another day under the knowledge! By
tonight they'll hear out there how I died – and they'll believe

it's true! ... Let them forget me then. For the rest of time whenever men say Mozart with love, they will say Salieri with loathing!
... *I am going to be immortal after all!* And He is powerless to prevent
it! So, Signore – see now if Man is mocked!

[*The* VALET *comes in with a tray, bearing a bowl of hot shaving
water, soap and a razor. He sets this on the table.* SALIERI *hands
him the Confession.*]

[*To* VALET]: Good morning. Lay this on the desk in the Cabinet.
Append your name to it in witness that this is my hand. *Via –
subito!*

[*The man takes the paper and goes, bewildered, upstage right.* SALIERI
*picks up the razor and rises. He addresses the audience most
simply and directly.*]

Amici cari. I was born a pair of ears and nothing else. It is only
through hearing music that I know God exists. Only through
writing music that I could worship. All around me men seek
liberty for Mankind. I sought only slavery for myself. To be owned
– ordered – exhausted by an *Absolute.* This was denied me,
and with it all meaning.

[*He opens the razor.*]

Now I go to become a ghost myself. I will stand in the shadows
when you come here to this earth in your turn. And when you
feel the dreadful bite of your failures – and hear the taunting of
unachievable, uncaring God – I will whisper my name to you:
'Salieri: Patron Saint of Mediocrities!' And in the depth of your
downcastness you can pray to me. And I will forgive you. *Vi
saluto.*

[*He cuts his throat, and falls backwards into the wheelchair.*

The COOK – *who has just come in, carrying a plate of fresh buns
for breakfast – sees this and screams. The* VALET *rushes in at the same
time from the other side. Together they pull the wheelchair, with its
slumped body, backwards upstage, and anchor it in the centre.*

The VENTICELLI *appear again, in the costume of 1823.*]

VENTICELLO I: Beethoven's Conversation Book, eighteen twenty-
three. Visitors write the news for the deaf man.

[*He hands a book to* VENTICELLO 2.]

VENTICELLO 2 [*reading*]: 'Salieri has cut his throat – but is still alive!'

[SALIERI *stirs and comes to life, looking about him bewilderedly. The* VALET *and the* COOK *depart. He stares out front like an astounded gargoyle.*]

VENTICELLO 1: Beethoven's Conversation Book, eighteen twenty-four. Visitors write the news for the deaf man.

[*He hands another book to* VENTICELLO 2.]

VENTICELLO 2 [*reading*]: 'Salieri is quite deranged. He keeps claiming that he is guilty of Mozart's death, and made away with him by poison.'

[*The light narrows into a bright cone, beating on* SALIERI.]

VENTICELLO 1: The *German Musical Times*, May the twenty-fifth, eighteen twenty-five.

[*He hands a newspaper to* VENTICELLO 2.]

VENTICELLO 2 [*reading*]:'Our worthy Salieri just cannot die. In the frenzy of his imagination he is even said to accuse himself of complicity in Mozart's early death. A rambling of the mind believed in truth by no one but the deluded old man himself.'

[*The music stops.* SALIERI *lowers his head, conceding defeat.*]

VENTICELLO 1: I don't believe it.

VENTICELLO 2: I don't believe it.

[*They look in turn at Salieri.*]

VENTICELLO 1: I don't believe it.

VENTICELLO 2: I don't believe it.

VENTICELLO 1 *and* VENTICELLO 2: *No one believes it in the world!*

[*They go off. The light dims a little.* SALIERI *slowly rises and walks downstage: a lone figure in the darkness.*]

SALIERI: Mediocrities everywhere – now and to come – I absolve you all. Amen!

[*He extends his arms upwards and outwards to embrace the assembled audience in a wide gesture of Benediction – finally folding his arms high across his own breast.*

The light fades completely. The last four chords of the Masonic Funeral Music of AMADEUS MOZART *sound throughout the theatre.*]

END OF PLAY

SALIERI'S MARCH as played by both Salieri and Mozart, Mozart playing it faster, lighter, and less decoratively.

MOZART'S TRANSFORMATION PROCESS:

'It doesn't really work, that fourth – does it?'

'Let's try the third above...'   'Ah yes!...'

'NON PIÚ ANDRAI' arranged for piano by Kevin Leeman
At first tentatively

POSTSCRIPT:

THE PLAY AND THE FILM

The cinema is a worrying medium for the stage playwright to work in. Its unverbal essence offers difficulties to anyone living largely by the spoken word. Increasingly, as American films grow ever more popular around the world, it is apparent that the most successful are being spoken in Screen-speak, a kind of cinematic esperanto equally comprehensible in Bogotà and Bulawayo. For example, dialogue in heavy-action pictures, horrific or inter-galactic, now consists almost entirely of the alternation of two single words – a cry and a whisper – needing translation nowhere on the planet: *'Less-gidowaheer!'* and *'Omygaad!'* Mastery of this new tongue is not easy for older writers.

Equally dismaying has to be the endemic restlessness of film-goers. In his mind's ear as he writes for the live theatre, the dramatist can presume the attentiveness of his audience: its mutual agreement to listen, and to remain in one place while the performance is going on. No such agreement exists among movie audiences. Indeed the very word 'movies' nowadays can as accurately describe the viewers of films as films themselves. I never really understood the meaning of the phrase 'upward mobility' until I had ex-perienced a Manhattan cinema on a recent Saturday night.

All of which is by way of saying that but for the enthusiasm of Mr Milos Forman I doubt if there would be a film of *Amadeus* at all. He met me in London after the very first preview of the play at the National Theatre in November 1979, and declared without hesitation that what I had actually written was a natural film, and that if I were ever willing to let him do so, he would direct it. In this assertion he persisted for two years.

Persistence was coupled with perceptiveness. When finally I cautiously agreed to explore the possibility of working with him, he sensed quite plainly my unease about films in general, and my dissatisfaction with all previous films of my own plays in particular. When I asked him what he would do with my piece, he told me what he would *not* do: turn it into a stagey hybrid, neither play nor picture. He also pointed out that the film of a play is really a new work, another fulfilment of the same impulse which had created the original. The adapter's task was to explore many new paths in order to emerge in the end at the same emotional place. During this process a fair amount of demolition work would go on, some of it perhaps painful to the author. In the case of *Amadeus*, its operatic stylization would probably have to go, and its language would have to be made less formal, though not, of course, more juvenile.

Actually my own personal taste in cinema inclines very much to the operatic and stylized – the opening sequence of the *The Magnificent Ambersons*, for example, or the iconographic groupings in *Ivan the Terrible*, Part 1 – but I also sensed, as we talked, how this vigorous man's brand of naturalism, infused with his huge humour and his obvious passion for my material, might make an enthralling new thing out of it. The possibility of working with him was suddenly very tempting.

Certainly I was not afraid of new approaches. In composing the play I had spent over a year simply finding a way of beginning it. I don't know how many bewigged phantoms I chased down how many suddenly blocked avenues before settling on the final formulation. Why not join a brilliantly talented film director in even further exploration? Of course partnership would mean permitting him to write the script with me, alone in his house – the Forman method, and one not easy for an author to countenance – but I reckoned that I had ultimately far more to learn than to lose from such an adventure, and finally I agreed. On the first day of February 1982 our collaboration began.

It was a startling experience for me. In the end we spent well over four months together in a Connecticut farmhouse – five days a week, twelve hours a day – seeing virtually no other company. These were four months of sustained work, punctuated by innumerable tussles, falterings and depressions, but also by sudden gleeful breakthroughs to relieve the monotony of the prevalent uncertainty. In some ways we made an 'Odd Couple', yoked together in a temporary form of marriage, cooking for each other in the evenings, and each day exploring whatever might contribute a Variation on the vast theme of Mozart and Salieri. We acted out countless versions of each scene, improvising them aloud. I sat at a long refectory table extracting, writing down, and polishing all dialogue. In the process I filled at least twenty thick notebooks. Some of the talk is inevitably simpler in the film than in the play, but none of it, I hope, is Screenspeak. At my urging, Mr Forman set out to investigate an unfamiliar world of music; at his, Mr Shaffer set out to investigate an equally unfamiliar one of screen technique.

If nothing else were to come out of this frenzied seclusion, we each discovered a new discipline and a new friendship.

From the start we agreed upon one thing: we were not making an objective Life of Wolfgang Mozart. This cannot be stressed too strongly. Obviously *Amadeus* on stage was never intended to be a documentary biography of the composer, and the film is even less of one. Certainly we have incorporated many real elements, new as well as true. The film shows the acerbic relationship between the fretful young genius and his haughty employer, Archbishop Colloredo of Salzburg; the disastrous visit of Papa Leopold to his married son in Vienna; Wolfgang's playing of his Piano Concerti in the open air; his delight in dancing and billiards. But we are also blatantly claiming the grand licence of the storyteller to embellish his tale with fictional ornament and, above all, to supply it with a climax whose sole justification need be that it enthralls his audience and emblazons his theme. I believe that we have created just such a climax for the film of *Amadeus*.

To me there is something pure about Salieri's pursuit of an eternal Absolute through music, just as there is something irredeemably impure about his simultaneous pursuit of eternal fame. The yoking of these two clearly opposed drives led us finally to devise a climax totally different from that of the play: a night-long encounter between the physically dying Mozart and the spiritually ravenous Salieri, motivated entirely by the latter's crazed lust to snatch a piece of divinity for himself. Such a scene quite obviously never took place in fact. However, our concern at this point was not with fact but with the undeniable laws of drama. It is where, holding fast to the thread of our protagonist's mania, we were finally led.

Some people may find this new climax hard to accept. Others may rejoice in it as a horribly logical end to the legend. To me it seems the most appropriate finish to our black fantasia. Even on stage I had to create a final confrontation quite outside historical record. I had to recognize and honour the change of atmosphere from clear Enlightenment to murky Gothic which inevitably occurred once the figure of the Masked Messenger was introduced. In the film this recognition is more carefully prepared for. Indeed the motif of masked people goes all through the picture – paralleling to some extent Mozart's own preoccupation with them. After all, the three great Da Ponte operas are all concerned with the dramatic effects of wearing disguise.

What pleased me best about this resolution is that we were able to construct a scene which is highly effective in cinematic terms, yet wholly concerned with the least visual of all possible subjects: *music itself*. I do not believe that a stage version of this scene would have been half as effective.

Filming *Amadeus* for six months in Czechoslovakia was a testing but perhaps indispensable experience, considering our subject. Prague offers the most complete Baroque and Rococo setting in Europe, largely untouched by the savageries of war or city planners. It is possible to turn a camera there in a complete circle and see in its frame nothing built after Mozart's death. Architecturally, Czech buildings provide a perfect background for the story, just as aesthetically Czech faces provide a perfect foreground. The people of Central Europe are not embarrassed by wearing period costume: the smallest bit-player on a day's leave from the factory looks absolutely natural in perruque and pelisse. Contemplating the audiences of extras assembled in the Tyl theatre to watch the Mozart operas being played – the very theatre where *Don Giovanni* was first produced! – one experiences the miraculous feeling of time being reclaimed from oblivion. I hope profoundly that this eerie and exquisite sensation will seep through the print on to the screen.

What I hope will not seep through is any sense of the difficulties experienced in making the picture. These of course were considerable. Inevitably the very act of making a two-and-a-half-hour costume picture entirely behind the Iron Curtain became something of an ordeal for all concerned. I keep meeting people who imagine that the business of setting up cameras and turning them on sets and actors is somehow a romantic and liberating occupation. It is impossible to convince them that the daily activity of a camera crew is just about as liberating as that of Sisyphus. On each visit I grew more and more impressed by the sheer staying-power of everyone concerned: by the manner in which a hundred different skills were kept keen and shining in the face of all that could blunt and rust them. Throughout what seemed an interminable time (for the river of Time unquestionably flows through the channels of Czechoslovakia more slowly than it does elsewhere) the producer, Saul Zaentz, defied all known rules laid down for the behaviour of movie producers by presenting each morning to the world of delay and confusion a countenance of unalterable equanimity.

I am extremely grateful to him for this example of poise, as I am to the entire team for its endurance, and above all to Milos Forman for showing me how you can hold every detail of a long film in your head simultaneously for six frenzied months – provided that you have first prepared it properly over another six. Fine directors do not appear by accident, nor do fine pictures.

Nevertheless, despite this and all his other dazzling demonstrations to me, which may yet result one day in my attempting an original film script, our joint movie is definitely the first and last of the metamorphoses of *Amadeus*. Unlike *Equus* it will not also become a ballet; unlike *The Royal Hunt of the*

Sun it will not become an opera. Above all, and no matter how fortunate our effort may prove in its reception, it will spawn no sequels. There will be no television series of half-hour dramas in which Salieri plots a different method of murdering Mozart each week, only to be frustrated by the wily little genius in the twenty-ninth minute. Even Mr Forman will agree that there can be a limit to adaptation.

PETER SHAFFER